Chuck and Blanche Johnson's

Savor™ Portland Cookbook

Portland's Finest Restaurants Their Recipes & Their Histories

Wilderness Adventures Press, Inc.
Belgrade, Montana

This book was manufactured with an easy-open, lay-flat binding.

Published by Wilderness Adventures Press, Inc.™
45 Buckskin Road
Belgrade, MT 59714
1-800-925-3339
Web site: www.wildadv.com
E-mail: books@wildadvpress.com
First Edition

Chuck and Blanche Johnson's Savor™ Cookbook Series

Printed in the United States of America

Library of Congress Cataloging-in-Publication Data

Johnson, Chuck.
Chuck and Blanche Johnson's Savor Portland cookbook : Portland's finest restaurants, their recipes and their histories.
p. cm.
Includes index.
ISBN 1-932098-18-6
1. Cookery. 2. Restaurants–Oregon–Portland–Guidebooks. I. Johnson, Blanche, 1943- II. Title.

TX714.J5986 2004
641.5'0979549–dc22

2004020582

ISBN 1-932098-18-6

Table of Contents

Portland Harbor - 1872.
Inset: Battleship Oregon.

Introduction

The city of Portland, Oregon is a gem in a state that boasts some of the most beautiful places in the United States. The city is a joy in which to travel, given its many user-friendly modes of transportation, and its gracious residents who always seem to be happy to help the neophyte traveler. It is a city that is growing in sophistication, yet retaining it's friendly small-town Western roots. With its close proximity to the Willamette Valley, Portland restaurants are blessed with some of the best and freshest produce in the country, as well as direct access to producers of fish, meats, and game.

In this, the fourth travel cookbook in our Savor Series, we had the pleasure of exploring the town and meeting with many of its top chefs and restaurant owners. We had purposefully left Portland out of our "Savor Oregon Cookbook" because we were aware of the growing reputation of Portland's culinary stars. The attention that the James Beard Foundation has paid to the Portland area chefs is testimony enough. In this book we are proud to present some of the best chefs and restaurants in the area.

It is important to note that all of the featured restaurants were by invitation. None of the restaurants are charged for appearing in the book. We selected them based on the excellence and uniqueness of their food, as well as their ambience. Many have interesting histories. We also looked for places that feature wines; especially Oregon wines. The Oregon Historical Museum provided interesting historical photographs of Portland that are scattered throughout the book, along with photos from the restaurants and from our own cameras.

The reader can use this book in several ways. As a travel guide, the reader can learn something about a restaurant's history, philosophy, and ambience, as well as the type of cuisine that it features. The map in the front gives the reader a perspective of the city and approximately where each restaurant is located.

Reading the recipes is a fun way to get a "taste" of each restaurant, and trying them out at home can be fun for the home chef as well his or her guests. Over 125 delicious recipes are featured, giving a wide variety to suit all tastes.

Blanche and Chuck Johnson

Portland Hotel SW 6th Avenue ca. 1910.
Inset: Saxer Brewery 1860.

ACKNOWLEDGMENTS

We would like to give our special thanks to the owners, managers, and chefs of the featured restaurants for their help in gathering the information for this book, as well as their generosity in sharing some of their favorite recipes with us.

The magazine, Northwest Palate, was a valuable resource in keeping us up to date with the restaurants and wineries of the Northwest.

Our appreciation extends to the gracious staff of the Oregon Historical Society. They were a great aid in helping us find historic photographs to add to this book.

We also want to give recognition to our graphic designer, Mark Woodward, and to our project manager and editor, Lynn Kinnaman, for their efforts in bringing this project to fruition.

Savor™ Portland Cookbook

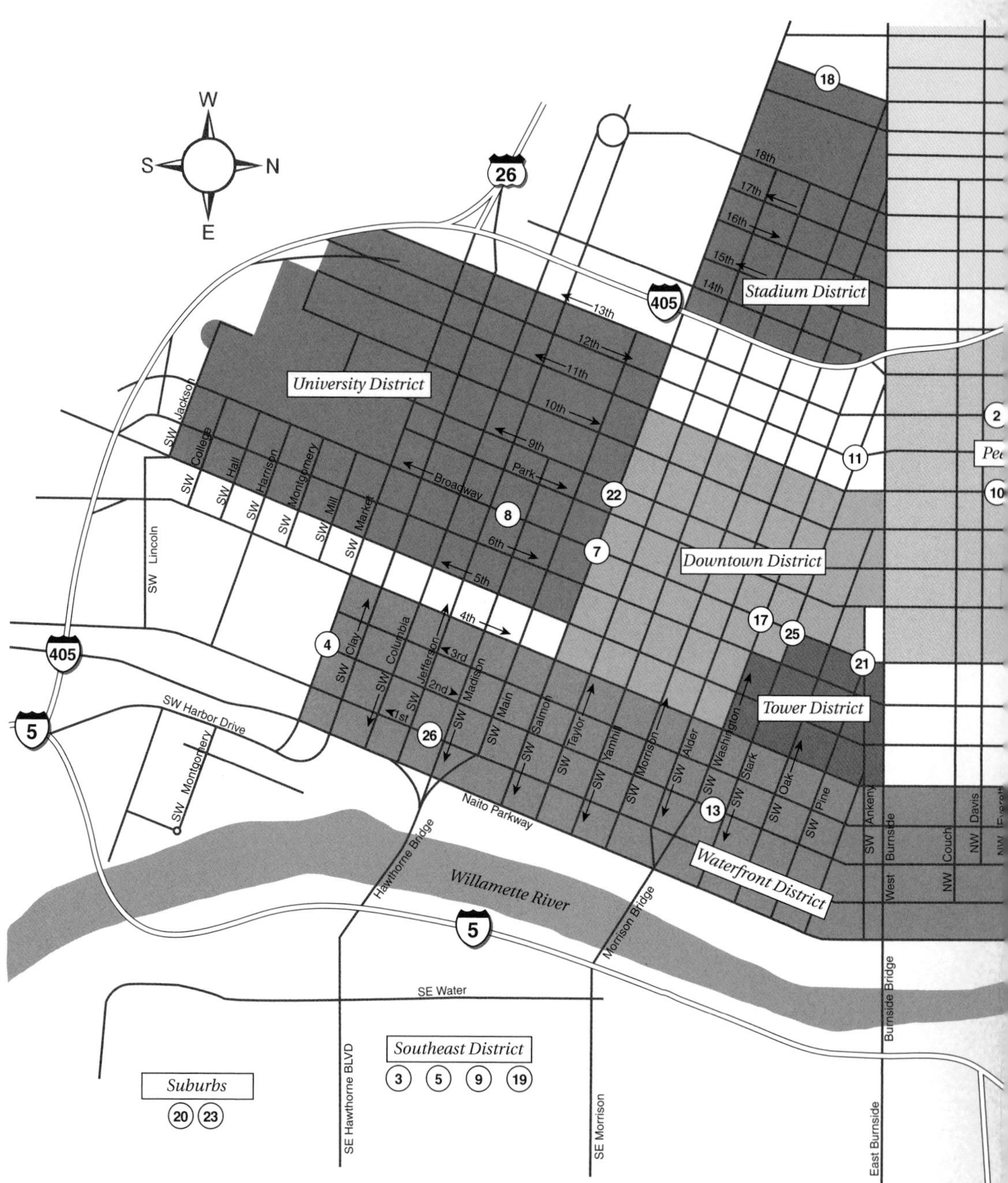

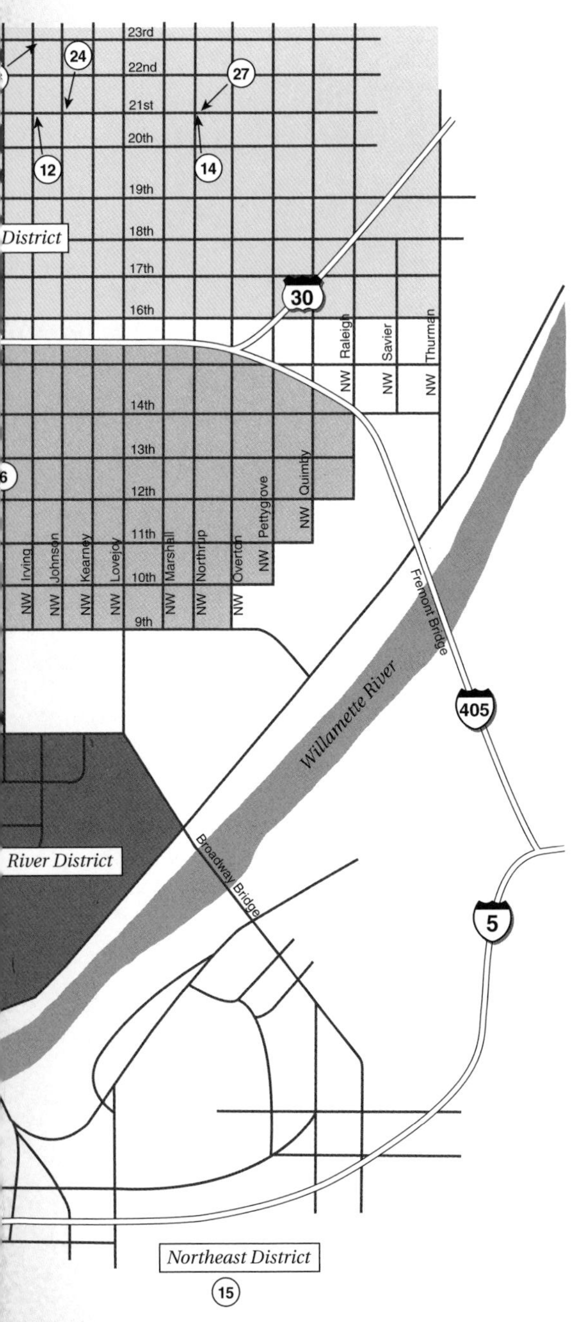

Featured Restaurants

1. andina
2. Bluehour
3. Caprial's
4. Carafe
5. Castagna
6. Fratelli
7. Heathman
8. Higgins
9. Il Piatto
10. In Good Taste
11. Jake's Famous Crawfish
12. Lucy's Table
13. Mother's Bistro
14. Paley's Place
15. Pambiche
16. Papa Haydn
17. Pazzo Ristorante
18. Plainfield's Mayur
19. Sala
20. Salvador Molly's
21. Saucebox
22. Southpark Seafood Grill
23. Tucci
24. Tuscany Grill
25. Typhoon
26. Veritable Quandary
27. Wildwood

Portland Facts

Colonel Theodore Roosevelt.

Date Incorporated: Portland was incorporated in 1851 by the territory of Oregon, eight years prior to the year Oregon was granted statehood, 1859. In 1903, the State of Oregon granted a new Charter to the City of Portland.
Elevation: 173 feet above sea level
Population (cert. est. 2003): 545,140
Land Area: 130 square miles

Largest Employers: Largest employers include Nike, Intel, and Oregon Health and Science University.

Major industry: Tourism, high-tech, health care and manufacturing.

Nation's Smallest Designated Park: Mill Ends Park, 24 square inches in size

Park and Green Spaces: 37,000 acres, including the 5,000-acre Forest Park, the nation's largest urban wilderness.

Portlandia.

Fun Facts About Portland:
Portland is considered an example of outstanding urban planning. The city is known as The City of Roses.

Portland's International Rose Test Garden, located high above the city, is the oldest in the nation and features more than 500 varieties of roses cultivated continuously since 1917.

The Oregon Brewers Festival is the largest gathering of independent brewers in North America. Portland is known as the epicenter of America's craft brewing renaissance, with 40 microbreweries and brewpubs located in the Portland area.

In 1852 Henry Saxer established the Liberty Brewery in downtown Portland, near First and Davis Streets.

The Port of Portland's combined terminals handle $10.5 billion worth of cargo each year.

Carafe

200 SW Market Street
Portland, OR 97201
503-248-0004
www.carafebistro.com

Monday – Thursday
11:00 am – 10:00 pm
Friday
11:00 am – 11:00 pm
Saturday
5:00 pm – 11:00 pm
Sunday
4:00 pm – 9:00 pm

Carafe

Husband and wife team, Pascal Sauton and Julie Hunter, opened Carafe in August 2003. Pascal was a Parisian native and served his apprenticeship at the renowned three-star restaurant, Lasserre, in Paris. In 1985 he came to the U.S. and worked as the executive chef of The Pear & Partridge Inn in Bucks County, PA. Later he ran the kitchen at the Fourth Story Restaurant in Denver, and most recently he was the executive chef at Lucere in the Riverplace Hotel in Portland. Before opening Carafe, Julie Hunter served as the Catering Manager at Pearl District culinary store, In Good Taste. At Carafe she runs the front of the house, and along with Pascal, has created a fine wine list featuring wines from France and the Northwest.

Carafe is a Parisian-style bistro featuring traditional bistro fare in a lively atmosphere. As Pascal is quoted, "A bistro must be French, small, noisy and jovial, with inexpensive, classic dishes". The space that Carafe occupies has been turned into a perfect model of a French bistro, with its terrazzo tile floors, comfortable bentwood and cane chairs and its floor-to-ceiling windows with lace half-curtains. Bottles of French wines are displayed on the backs of the leather banquets. Outside seating is available with the same comfortable chairs. Located downtown, across from Keller Auditorium, the bistro is placed perfectly for those who are attending a concert or play, as well as for those who simply enjoy seeing the well-dressed attendees. Situated on the outside of the parking garage, Carafe offers complimentary valet parking at night.

Pascal works closely with the best local organic farmers and producers and his daily menus are based around the day's deliveries of northwest seafood, meats and produce. Pascal is a cooking artist who stays true to classic dishes while incorporating local foods that are new to classic French fare. Servers leave the kitchen knowing each ingredient and its flavors, because Pascal has made sure they are educated on, and have tasted, the food.

Warm Hood River Asparagus with Morels and Poached Duck Egg

Ingredients

2 tablespoons aged sherry vinegar
6 tablespoons walnut oil
1 teaspoon truffle oil
fleur de sel (sea salt) and black pepper
1 bunch asparagus, trimmed and peeled
1 tablespoon extra virgin olive oil
1 cup fresh morels
1 cup vegetable stock
4 duck eggs
2 quarts water
2 tablespoons white wine vinegar
1 tablespoon chives, finely minced
sea salt, black peppercorns for garnish

Preparation

FOR the vinaigrette, combine the sherry vinegar, walnut oil, truffle oil, salt, and black pepper, and whisk vigorously to blend well together, set aside until serving.

BLANCH the asparagus in salted boiling water until bright in color and still crunchy (2 to 3 minutes). Once done, cool in an ice bath, and drain on paper towels and lightly brush with olive oil.

TRIM the morels and wash quickly in cold clear water. Bring the vegetable stock to a boil, and poach the morels on a low simmer for 5 to 8 minutes. Drain and reserve.

FOR the poached eggs, bring two quarts of water to a boil in a saucepan with the vinegar. Turn the heat down and keep on a simmer. Crack the eggs and add to the water. Cook until the white is firm but the yolk still runny.

WHILE the eggs are cooking, warm the asparagus lightly under the broiler or in a hot oven. Place the asparagus on 4 plates with the morels on top. When the eggs are done, remove from water with a slotted spoon and place on top of asparagus and morels. Sprinkle a little bit of fleur de sel (sea salt) on top and some crushed black peppercorns.
Drizzle with the vinaigrette and the chives.

Serves 4

Navarin d'Agneau Printanier (Spring Lamb Stew)

Ingredients

- 1½ *pounds boneless lamb shoulder, cut in 3-ounce cubes*
- *sea salt*
- *black pepper*
- 2 *tablespoons olive oil*
- 1 *cup diced onions*
- 4 *garlic cloves, peeled and sliced*
- 3 *thyme sprigs*
- 1 *bay leaf*
- *parsley stems*
- ½ *bottle dry white wine*
- 4 *tablespoons tomato paste*
- 1 *quart veal stock*
- 1 *pound new potatoes*
- 8 *baby turnips*
- 8 *baby carrots*
- 1 *cup English peas, peeled and blanched*
- 8 *asparagus, peeled and blanched*
- 16 *pearl onions*
- 1 *tablespoon butter*
- 1 *tablespoon sugar*
- 3 *tablespoons parsley, chopped*

Preparation

SEASON the lamb cubes with salt and pepper. Heat the oil in a cocotte and sear the lamb in it. Remove.

PLACE the onions, garlic, thyme, bay leaf, and parsley in the cocotte, and cook for a minute.

ADD the meat and deglaze with the white wine.

REDUCE the wine until almost dry, add the tomato paste and the veal stock.

COOK, covered, at a simmer for an hour and a half. Check seasoning. Remove the onions, garlic, thyme, bay leaf, and parsley.

PEEL the potatoes, turnips, and carrots and cut in even sizes. Cook in salted boiling water to three-quarters done. Add to the lamb 15 minutes before it is done, along with the peas and asparagus.

PEEL the pearl onions and glaze with butter and sugar for 5 minutes. Garnish with chopped parsley.

Serves 4

Canard aux Olives

Ingredients

4 legs of duck confit
2 tablespoons duck fat
1 cup pancetta, finely diced
¼ cup sliced shallots
1 tablespoon sliced garlic
1 sprig rosemary, chopped
8 pitted green olives, cut in half
8 pitted black olives, cut in half
1 cup dry white wine
2 tablespoons extra virgin olive oil

Preparation

IN A large, heavy sauté pan, heat the duck fat. Add the duck legs, skin side down. Cover with an aluminum foil and place in the oven until the skin is crisp.

REMOVE the duck, and most of the fat, and add the pancetta. Cook until the pancetta starts crisping and add shallots, garlic, rosemary, and olives. Cook for 2 minutes, then add the white wine. Reduce by half and whisk in the olive oil.

CHECK seasoning, and serve immediately.

Serves 2

Cassoulet

Ingredients

- 1½ pounds Tarbais, Coco Blanc, or Scarlet Runner beans
- water to cover
- ½ cup duck fat
- 1 pork and garlic sausage such as Cottechino or Toulouse
- 4 1-ounce pieces of lightly smoked bacon or Ganciale
- 2 yellow onions, diced small
- 2 tablespoons sliced garlic
- 1 teaspoon fresh thyme
- 1 bay leaf
- 1 cup white wine
- 1 gallon lamb braising liquid or light veal stock
- 1 large can tomatoes
- salt and pepper to taste
- 6 ounces duck confit meat, skinless, boneless
- 8 ounces braised lamb meat, boneless
- 2 tablespoons duck fat
- 1 cup bread crumbs
- 2 tablespoons parsley, chopped

Preparation

SOAK the beans overnight in cold water. To cook, start the beans in cold water. Bring to a boil, drain, then replace the cold water, bring to a boil again, and simmer until the beans are tender.

TO MAKE the stock, take a large pot and heat the duck fat. Sear the sausages and bacon on all sides in the duck fat. Remove. Add the onions, garlic, thyme, and bay leaf, and cook until the onions start turning brown. Add the white wine, stock, and tomatoes. Bring to a boil and season with salt and pepper.

ADD the sausage, bacon, and beans and cook on a simmer for ½ hour. Remove the sausage and bacon and cut in service pieces. Leave the beans in the broth. Check seasoning.

WHEN ready to assemble, spread a layer of beans on the bottom of a baking dish. Add the duck confit, braised lamb, sausage, and bacon. Cover with another layer of beans. Make sure the beans are wet but not swimming in broth. (You may have to add some broth during the baking if the beans dry out too much.)

HEAT 2 tablespoons duck fat and toast the bread crumbs and chopped parsley in it. Sprinkle on top and bake in a 350 degree oven for 45 minutes.

Serves 4

7 *Carafe, Downtown*

Crepes Suzette

History of Crepes Suzette

The Crepe Suzette is probably the most famous crepe dish in the world. In a restaurant, a crepe suzette is often prepared in a chafing dish in full view of the guests. Crepes are served hot with a sauce of sugar, orange juice, and liqueur (usually Grand Marnier). Brandy is poured over the crepes and then lit.

The dish was created out of a mistake made by a fourteen year-old assistant waiter Henri Carpentier at the Maitre at Monte Carlo's Café de Paris in 1895. He was preparing a dessert for the Prince of Wales, the future King Edward VII (1841-1910) of England.

According to Henri Carpentier, in own words from Life A La Henri – Being The Memories of Henri Charpentier:

"It was quite by accident as I worked in front of a chafing dish that the cordials caught fire. I thought I was ruined. The Prince and his friends were waiting. How could I begin all over? I tasted it. It was, I thought, the most delicious melody of sweet flavors I had every tasted. I still think so. That accident of the flame was precisely what was needed to bring all those various instruments into one harmony of taste . . . He ate the pancakes with a fork; but he used a spoon to capture the remaining syrup. He asked me the name of that which he had eaten with so much relish. I told him it was to be called Crepes Princesse. He recognized that the pancake controlled the gender and that this was a compliment designed for him; but he protested with mock ferocity that there was a lady present. She was alert and rose to her feet and holding her little shirt wide with her hands she made him a curtsey. 'Will you,' said His Majesty, 'change Crepes Princesse to Crepes Suzette?' Thus was born and baptized this confection, one taste of which, I really believe, would reform a cannibal into a civilized gentleman. The next day I received a present from the Prince, a jeweled ring, a panama hat and a cane."

Ingredients

5 *navel oranges, juiced (about 1 cup orange juice)*
1 *tablespoon sugar*
2 *tablespoons orange liqueur, such as Grand Marnier*
6 *navel oranges, peeled and sectioned*
vanilla ice cream (optional)
Crepes (recipe follows)

Preparation

MAKE crepes, following directions below. When ready to assemble, place a large skillet over high heat, bring the orange juice to a boil. Add the sugar, reduce to medium heat, and simmer for 2 minutes.

REMOVE from heat and add the orange liqueur and orange sections. Set aside.

WORKING in batches, gently place a crepe, folded into fourths, into the pan holding the orange juice and orange sections. Leave for 1 minute to absorb some juice.

USING a narrow spatula, remove the crepe to a warm serving plate. Spoon on some orange sections and sauce. Top with vanilla ice cream and serve immediately.

For the Crepes

4 *eggs*
1 *cup all purpose flour*
1 *cup milk*
½ *cup water*
3 *tablespoons sugar*
¼ *teaspoon salt*
2 *ounces butter, melted*

HOMOGENIZE all ingredients in a blender, incorporating hot melted butter at the end. Do not over mix. Strain through a fine mesh strainer and chill for at least 2 hours. Use a one ounce ladle for a 7" diameter crepe. Pour one ounce into hot pan to make crepe, then set aside until needed.

Yields about 25 crepes

Lewis & Clark Exposition grand staircase, 1905.

The Heathman Restaurant & Bar

Located in the Heathman Hotel, next door to the Arlene Schnitzer Concert Hall, The Heathman Restaurant offers one of the best dining experiences in Portland. The main dining room sports large windows overlooking busy Salmon Street, and is usually filled with convivial diners enjoying the daily selections presented by Executive Chef Philippe Boulot. For those who may want a quieter setting, dining is also available in The Lobby Bar. This is a beautiful 2-story high room that has been painstakingly restored to its former splendor. On cool evenings, the large marble fireplace boasts a cheery fire that lights the handsome eucalyptus paneled walls. The Steinway grand piano sits below the grand staircase and sets the stage for an evening of live jazz performances that are held regularly. Service in either dining room is impeccable.

A native of Normandy, Executive Chef Philippe Boulot is a graduate of the Jean Drouant Hotel School in Paris. After graduating, Chef Boulot traveled extensively, working in some of the world's finest hotels, including The Nikko in Paris, the Four Seasons Inn on The Park in London, as well as the Four Seasons Cliff Hotel in San Francisco and The Mark Hotel in New York. In 1994, Chef Boulot joined The Heathman and has created a special niche for himself in the Pacific Northwest, and has done much to increase Portland's reputation as a city of fine restaurants. His classic French training and love of the local produce has allowed him to create his own style of "French Northwest".

Through this "Philippe's Friends" program, Chef Boulot brings world-renowned chefs to The Heathman Restaurant to share their expertise. Visiting chefs join him in developing special prix fixe menus to the delight of restaurant patrons. In turn, he travels to other venues, including the James Beard House, to offer his culinary knowledge to others.

In 2001, Chef Boulot won the coveted James Beard Award of "Best Chef of the Pacific Northwest. He and his talented kitchen staff have earned The Heathman many awards over the last ten years, including Gourmet Magazine's 1997 honor as one of the "Top Ten Tables in Portland". In 1995, Conde Nast listed The Heathman as one of the "Top 250 Restaurants in America". But, don't be influenced just by the amount of awards that have been bestowed on the restaurant. Come visit The Heathman and find out for yourself . Look for Chef Phillippe's upcoming cookbook.

Award of Excellence

Foie Gras Cappuccino with Wild Mushrooms

Ingredients

- 4 *ounces Port wine*
- 8 *ounces duck foie gras, cut on bias into equal sized medallions*
- 4 *ounces wild mushrooms, chanterelles black trumpets or, morels or chanterelles*
- 2 *tablespoons shallots, peeled and sliced*
- 1 *tomato, seeded and chopped*
- ⅓ *cup heavy cream, whipped*
- *salt and pepper to taste*
- *Beef and Mushroom Stock (recipe follows)*

Preparation

PREPARE the beef and mushroom stock. To make the cappuccino soup, add reduced port wine to 1 cup of the beef and mushroom stock and heat to boiling in a saucepan. Adjust to taste with salt and pepper.

SAUTÉ foie gras medallions over medium-high heat until browned on both sides; place one medallion each in four bowls.

SAUTÉ wild mushrooms and sliced shallots in foie gras drippings until caramelized. Toss with chives and season to taste with salt and pepper.

TO SERVE, place cooked mushrooms in bowls on top of seared foie gras. Sprinkle diced tomato evenly among bowls. While soup is boiling, add the whipped cream, whisking to create foam. Pour the foamy cappuccino soup over mushrooms and foie gras, and serve immediately. For a dramatic presentation, pour the soup over the mushrooms and foie gras at tableside.

For the Beef and Mushroom Stock

- 2 *cups chicken stock*
- ¼ *cup onion, chopped*
- *mushroom stems and trimmings, chopped*
- *beef trimmings, chopped*
- 2 *tablespoons olive oil*
- *salt and pepper to taste*

CHOP onion, beef trimmings, and mushroom stems and trimmings. Sauté onion and trimmings in olive oil over medium high heat until well browned. Deglaze with chicken stock. Keep at a low boil until reduced by half. Strain through a fine sieve, season to taste with salt and pepper.

Serves 4

Cauliflower Vichyssoise

with Dungeness Crab, Horseradish Lime Sauce and Chive Oil

This soup is richly textured with wonderful sweet, earthy flavors of the cauliflower in counterpoint to the succulent, zingy flavors of the crab and horseradish sauce. This is good in the fall with just-picked cauliflower and fresh-caught crab. It is an elegant starting dish, or can be a simple supper.

Ingredients

- 1 *cauliflower head, large*
- 1 *bunch young leeks with lots of white*
- 1 *quart heavy cream*
- 1 *cup Dungeness crabmeat, cooked and cleaned*
- 4 *ounces butter*
- 1 *bay leaf*
- *salt and pepper*
- *Lime Horseradish Cream (recipe follows)*
- *Chive Oil (recipe follows)*

Preparation

CLEAN and trim head of cauliflower. Cut into medium-sized pieces. Trim root end of leeks and remove dark green part. Cut leeks in half lengthwise and rough chop them. Soak leeks in cold water to remove sand and dirt.

IN A clean soup kettle, melt butter over medium heat. Add leeks and cook until soft, but not browned. Add cauliflower and heavy cream and cook at a simmer until the cauliflower is thoroughly soft.

PUREE the soup in a blender or food processor and strain through sieve with medium holes. Chill completely. Season with salt and pepper. Soup should have a thick and smooth consistency.

MAKE the lime horseradish cream, add crabmeat and toss to coat.

SERVE soup cold in a chilled serving bowl. Spoon soup into bowl. Divide crab mixture and place on top of soup. Drizzle chive oil.

For the Lime Horseradish Cream

- ⅓ *cup sour cream*
- 2 *tablespoons horseradish, grated*
- *juice of one lime*
- *zest of two limes*

COMBINE all ingredients in a bowl.

For the Chive Oil

1 bunch chives
¼ cup olive oil, fruity spicy style

COMBINE chives and olive oil and process thoroughly in a blender. Strain through a fine sieve.

Serves 2–4

Dungeness Crab and Mango Salad

with Citrus Vinaigrette

Ingredients

8 ounces Dungeness crab meat, cooked and cleaned
4 blood oranges, juiced
2 limes, juiced
1 lemon, juiced
¼ cup olive oil
2 mangoes, peeled, pitted and diced small
2 avocados, peeled, pitted and diced small
1 cup micro greens or alfalfa sprouts
1 3" diameter pipe section about 3" long, from hardware store

Preparation

TO PREPARE the vinaigrette, combine orange, lemon, and lime juices in a pan and simmer on the stovetop to reduce by volume to just ¼ cup.

COOL reduced fruit juice, and add olive oil. Add a pinch of salt and a scant pinch of cayenne pepper. Whisk to emulsify. Toss crabmeat, mango, and avocado with vinaigrette.

TO SERVE, place pipe section in middle of plate. Pack into equal layer in pipe section firmly, so salad will hold its shape when pipe is removed. Top with portion of sprouts or micro greens and remove pipe to serve. Drizzle rest of vinaigrette around the salad.

Serves 4

Orange Crusted Sea Scallops

with Organic Tomato Compote and Grapefruit Beurre Fondue

The sweet-bitter flavor of the orange zest is a surprising and delicious addition to the creamy, sweet flesh of the scallops. The compote and grapefruit beurre fondue provide contrasting textures and flavors that both complement the crunchy crust. Avoid overcooking them to retain the best texture.

Ingredients

- *16 scallops, large*
- *4 oranges, zest*
- *simple syrup (½ cup water + ½ cup sugar)*
- *⅓ cup panko bread crumbs*
- *2 tablespoons olive oil*
- *Organic Tomato Compote (recipe follows)*
- *Grapefruit Beurre Fondue (recipe follows)*

Preparation

ZEST the oranges, taking care to avoid the white pith. In a small pot, simmer the zest in the simple syrup until very soft. Strain to recover orange zest.

PLACE the orange zest on a baking sheet and bake in a 195-degree oven until very dry. Mix orange zest with panko bread crumbs in a blender blend well.

ROLL the scallops in the zest and bread crumb mixture until well coated. Heat olive oil in a sauté pan over medium-high heat. Cook until seared on both sides, turning once. Set aside and keep warm. Make the tomato compote and grapefruit beurre fondue.

TO SERVE, take a soup plate, place tomato compote in the center and top with seared scallops. Drizzle grapefruit beurre fondue around.

For the Organic Tomato Compote

- *4 organic tomatoes, chopped*
- *1 clove garlic, minced*
- *1 shallot, peeled and chopped*
- *2 tablespoons olive oil*
- *2 tablespoons Champagne vinegar*
- *salt and pepper to taste*
- *1 teaspoon parsley, minced fine*
- *1 teaspoon basil, minced fine*

IN A sauté pan, combine chopped tomatoes (without the core), garlic, and shallot with the olive oil, stirring often. Add vinegar and reduce until thick.

SCOOP tomato mixture into blender or food processor and puree. Season to taste with salt, pepper, parsley, and basil.

For the Grapefruit Beurre Fondue

1 cup grapefruit juice, fresh squeezed
⅓ cup butter
salt and pepper to taste

IN A small saucepan, reduce the grapefruit juice to ¼ cup. Stir in the butter and season to taste with salt and pepper

Serves 4

Potato Crusted Steelhead

Leek Compote, Wild Mushrooms, Red Wine Beurre Fondue

Wild steelhead trout are a favorite of sport fisherman because they put up one heck of a fight. Their cold-water existence also gives them a delicate, pink flesh with unforgettable flavor and texture. In this recipe the potato provides a crispy, light crust that complements the hearty meat of the fish, while the butter fondue and leek compote provide creamy and piquant notes to complete the dish. If you can't find steelhead, salmon filets make a terrific alternative. Prepare the leek compote and beurre fondue first, and then cook the fish.

Ingredients

4 6-ounce fillets, bones removed
4 Yukon Gold potatoes
1 cup butter
salt and pepper
Leek Compote (recipe follows)
Beurre Fondue (recipe follows)

Preparation

MAKE leek compote and beurre fondue. Preheat oven to 375 degrees. Peel potatoes and slice to a fine julienne, ⅛" on a side. Season fish fillets with salt and pepper. Add one tablespoon butter to non stick small sauté pan and heat to medium. Cover bottom of pan with a single layer of potatoes, closely packed. Place fish, flesh side down, on top of the potatoes. Add more potatoes, closely packed, layering on top of the fish. Cook until the potatoes begin to crust, showing good coloration. With plastic spatula, flip fish and cook until both sides are browned. Remove and place on well-oiled baking sheet if the fish is not cooked and finish cooking in the oven until the fish is cooked to your desired temperature.

TO SERVE, place warm leek compote in center of the plate. Top with potato crusted fish. Drizzle beurre fondue around the compote. We also serve this dish with sautéed wild mushrooms.

Potato Crusted Steelhead, continued

For the Leek Compote

6 leeks, medium sized
4 tablespoon butter
salt and pepper to taste

REMOVE outer leaves from leeks then chop and wash to clean dirt from between the layers. Melt butter on medium heat in saucepan. Add leeks, salt, and pepper. Cook slowly, lowering heat if necessary so as not to burn the vegetable, until leeks are soft. A small amount of water may be added if the compote begins to dry and leeks are not yet soft. Can be made in advance and reheated just before serving.

For the Beurre Fondue

2 cups red wine
¼ cup port
2 tablespoons heavy cream
½ cup butter, hard
salt and freshly ground black pepper

IN A saucepan, combine the red wine and port, reduce to ¼ cup liquid. Add heavy cream. Bring to a boil, Lower heat to simmer. Add butter cut in small dice, whisking to incorporate. Adjust seasoning with salt and pepper. Set aside and keep warm.

Serves 4

Gigot de Sept Heures

Seven Hour Leg of Lamb

Lamb cooked with this slow braise is fork-tender and very savory. The seasonings and wine cook down into a rich, velvety sauce that is packed with flavor. It's a one-dish meal, although you'll need a large Dutch oven or other oven-proof pan with a lid. Plan this meal in advance. You need one full day to marinate the lamb, and another day to rest the meat after the braise. This is a party meal that will easily serve eight adults.

Ingredients

1 leg of lamb, bone in
½ cup garlic, ground
¼ cup olive oil
2 each yellow onions, chopped
4 each carrots, chopped
2 stalk celery, chopped
1 teaspoon fresh rosemary
1 teaspoon fresh thyme
1 teaspoon fresh ground black pepper
1 teaspoon coriander
1 teaspoon juniper berries
2 bay leaves
1 sprig parsley
¼ cup flour
2 tablespoons tomato paste
1 bottle red wine
½ gallon water
salt and pepper to taste

Preparation

RUB lamb with the ground garlic and season liberally with salt and pepper. Marinate the lamb with seasonings for a full day in the refrigerator. Remove lamb from refrigerator; scrape off and set aside the ground garlic.

PLACE the leg of lamb in a large Dutch oven or other oven-proof pan. The pan should be large enough for the lamb to be covered with braising liquid, but not too much larger than the lamb. Heat oven to 450 and thoroughly brown the lamb in the oven, turning once. Remove pan from oven and set the leg of lamb aside.

LARGE dice all of the vegetables and combine with the reserved garlic. Heat the olive oil over medium heat on the stove top, using the same Dutch oven or large pan. Cook the vegetables until they start to brown. Stir in the flour and continue to cook until the flour is a toasted color. Stir in the tomato paste and cook briefly. Deglaze pan with red wine, and bring to a boil. Add the water, return the liquid to a boil, and remove from heat. Add all of the herbs and the reserved garlic.

ADJUST oven temperature to 250 degrees. Place the leg of lamb in the braising liquid and adjust, if necessary, so that the lamb is completely submerged. Cover the pan with a lid or seal tightly with foil and place in oven. Adjust oven temperature so that the braising liquid is at a very slow simmer, and cook for seven hours.

REMOVE the pan from the oven, and set aside the leg of lamb. Strain the braising liquid through a fine sieve and return to pan. Reduce the sauce if desired, or thin with water to desired consistency. Adjust seasonings with salt and pepper.

REMOVE bone and fat from cooked lamb, and place it back into the finished sauce to rest for 12 hours. Reheat the lamb and sauce together on the stovetop prior to serving.

TO SERVE, place portions of lamb, with generous quantity of sauce, in a large bowl or deep dinner plate.

GOES well with potato gnocchi, pasta or roasted local fingerling potatoes and tomato persillade.

Serves 8

Wine suggestion: Accompany with Oregon pinot noir or Washington merlot.

Braised Rabbit Normande

Rabbit is one of my favorite meats. It is flavorful and tender, and is terrific paired with many sauces and prepared by many different techniques. You can get rabbit hind pieces at any good butcher; save some effort and have them bone the rabbit, too. This is a classic preparation, like I used to do as a boy in Normandy for big family dinners. The braising makes the meat exceptionally tender and the flavor of the apple cider in the braising liquid gives the meat and the sauce a subtle, delicious apple flavor. It's easy to adjust this recipe for more or fewer guests.

Ingredients

4 rabbit hind legs, bone removed and butterflied
1 cup rabbit meat, ground
1 rabbit liver, diced
2 bacon slices, diced
2 teaspoons tarragon
½ cup bread crumbs, soaked in ⅓ cup milk
salt and pepper
1 sheet caul fat
4 tablespoons olive oil
1 onion, chopped
2 carrots, chopped
1 celery stalk, chopped
4 tablespoons flour
2 tablespoons tomato paste
1 bottle sparkling apple cider
chicken stock
2 teaspoons fresh minced rosemary
2 teaspoons fresh minced thyme
½ tablespoon garlic, pressed

Preparation

COMBINE ground rabbit meat, liver, bacon, and tarragon in a food processor and process until mixture forms a paste. Combine paste with bread crumbs soaked in milk.
Divide bread crumb mixture and place ¼ of total inside each rabbit leg. Fold rabbit leg over to enclose stuffing, and wrap the leg with caul fat.

CHOOSE an oven-proof braising pan large enough to hold the stuffed rabbit legs and braising liquid. On the stovetop, heat olive oil in the braising pan over medium heat and sauté the rabbit legs until browned all over. Remove rabbit legs from pan.

ADD the onion, carrots, and celery to the pan and sauté until they start to brown. Add the flour and stir in thoroughly, cooking until the flour is light brown. Add the tomato paste and cook for another two minutes.
Deglaze the pan with the bottle of apple cider. Add the chicken stock and bring to a boil for one minute. Remove from heat and adjust salt and pepper.

ADD the rosemary, thyme, and garlic to the liquid. Place the browned rabbit legs in the liquid, making sure they are covered. Cover the pan with a lid or foil and place in a 250 degree oven. Adjust temperature to keep the liquid at a slow simmer.

WHEN the meat is done, remove pan from the oven and remove the rabbit legs from the pan. Strain the sauce through a sieve or cheesecloth and return to the pan. Adjust sauce thickness and seasoning. Return the rabbit legs to the liquid, and allow the to rest overnight in the liquid before reheating to serve.

TO SERVE, place a hind piece in a bowl with a generous quantity of sauce. Goes well with roasted potatoes or fresh pasta.

Serves 4

Roasted Farm-Raised Venison

Wrapped in Applewood Smoked Bacon with Huckleberry Grand Veneur Sauce

Fallow venison means meat from farm-raised animals. You can buy fallow venison online or from good butcher shops. The loin is the most tender cut available, but is sometimes sold untrimmed; save some effort by having the butcher trim it for you. You can vary the type of bacon used for this recipe, but get the best quality, locally-cured bacon you can find.

Ingredients

- *1½ pounds venison loin, 2-3" diameter, trimmed of silver skin*
- *½ pound Applewood smoked bacon, thinly sliced*
- *¼ pounds caul fat, soaked in water*
- *Huckleberry Grand Veneur Sauce (recipe follows)*
- *Acorn Squash (recipe follows)*
- *Mushrooms (recipe follows)*

Preparation

MAKE the huckleberry sauce, acorn squash, and mushrooms. Preheat oven to 450 degrees. Roll venison loins in bacon. Bacon slices should overlap each other. Wring out a piece of caul fat and lay it out flat. Wrap the bacon wrapped venison in the caul fat. Place venison loin in a roasting rack in a shallow pan, and place in oven. Reduce oven temperature immediately to 350 degrees. Roast to desired doneness as you would for beef.

TO SERVE, slice medallions of venison and alternate with squash slices and pom pom mushrooms around the center of the plate. Top with sauce.

Roasted Farm-Raised Venison, continued

For the Huckleberry Grand Veneur Sauce

¼ cup huckleberry jam
1 bottle Oregon Pinot Noir
¼ cup huckleberries, fresh or frozen
1 cup butter

TO BEGIN the sauce, heat huckleberry jam, and cook until slightly caramelized. Deglaze with the Pinot Noir, and reduce to syrup. Add the fresh huckleberries and cook until the berries are soft.

CUT butter into small dices and whisk into sauce. Keep sauce warm.

For the Acorn Squash

2 acorn squash
½ cup butter
½ cup brown sugar
½ cup whiskey bourbon
salt and pepper

CUT squash in half lengthwise. Scoop out seeds and use a sharp paring knife to remove skins. Slice across the short length about 1½" thick. In a pan large enough to hold all of the squash, melt butter over medium heat. Add the brown sugar and bourbon and whisk to combine. Add the sliced squash and cook until thoroughly tender. Set aside.

For the Mushrooms

2 pounds pom pom mushrooms
3 tablespoons olive oil
salt and pepper

LIGHTLY coat the mushrooms with oil and season with salt and pepper. Grill or sauté on both sides until done.

Serves 8

Pioneer Square.

Higgins

Higgins

1239 S.W. Broadway
Portland, OR 97205
503-222-9070
www.higgins.citysearch.com

Lunch
Monday – Friday
11:30 am - 2:00 pm
Dinner
5:00 pm - 10:30 pm

Higgins

In 1994 Greg Higgins, along with his partner Paul Mallory opened Higgins in downtown Portland. The restaurant is in a historic building with a tin ceiling and wood floors. From Higgins open kitchen, the chef can see every seat in the restaurant. Behind him, two windows expose the kitchen to passers-by on Jefferson Street. The two-level dining room features a light and airy section adjoining the open kitchen, with the lower level featuring the original elegant mahogany paneling and painted patterns on the ceiling. Both sections offer diners privacy for intimate conversations in a relaxed, yet convivial atmosphere. The restaurant features flavorful, bistro-style dishes served by attentive, well-informed servers.

Greg Higgins has been a pillar of the Portland culinary scene for many years. Prior to opening Higgins, he served as Executive Chef at the Heathman Hotel. An avid organic gardener, Greg grows his own herbs, vegetables and fruits, passing along his research of heirloom varieties to his growers. Greg Higgins' premise is that food is community - an idea that creates respect, commitment and responsibility from the farmer to the chef to the diner. "We're interested in nourishing and sustaining not only our customer's appetites but also the land and the quality of life we enjoy," says Higgins.

Higgins' cooking focuses on Pacific Northwest ingredients and traditional French techniques; incorporating an eclectic range of influences from around the world. This is a culmination of his culinary education, starting with his employment by a traditional Italian restaurant during his college years. After college, he headed for Europe, landing training experiences in Alsace and Burgundy. After returning to the U.S., he cooked in restaurants in Sun Valley and Seattle before settling in Portland.

Higgins has promoted Northwest regional cuisine around the world. He has been on numerous television cooking shows including PBS's "New American Cuisine."

Greg and his restaurant have received numerous awards, including the James Beard Foundation Award "American Express Best Chef: Northwest/Hawaii" in 2002. Higgins was voted one of the top three restaurants in Portland by Zagat's survey, and was also named "Restaurant of the Year, 2003" by The Oregonian's Annual Restaurant Guide.

Most importantly, you can expect to enjoy an exceptional meal in a warm and comfortable surrounding. Higgins knows how to work magic with textures and flavors.

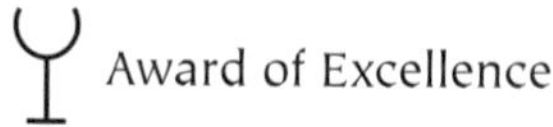

Oyster Stew
with Kippered Salmon, Leeks and Hard Cider

Ingredients

1 pint shucked oysters (extra small)
2 12-ounce bottles hard cider
2 cups Yukon Gold or Yellow Finn potatoes, peeled and diced ½"
1 pint heavy cream
2 leeks, diced ½ inch, cleaned well
6 ounces hot smoked "kippered" salmon, flaked
2 sprigs fresh thyme, leaves separated
salt and pepper to taste
squeeze of fresh lemon juice
dash of Tabasco
loaf of sourdough bread (optional)

Preparation

BRING the cider to a boil in a 2-3 quart non-reactive saucepan. Add the oysters and their liquid and cook for one minute. Using a slotted spoon, remove the oysters from the simmering cider and set them aside. Add the potatoes and cook until "al dente". Remove them from the broth and reduce the oyster poaching liquid 50% by boiling gently, about 15-20 minutes.

WHEN the liquid is reduced, add the heavy cream, the leeks, smoked salmon, oysters, potatoes, and fresh thyme. Bring the stew to a low simmer, stirring gently. Adjust the seasoning to taste with salt and pepper, lemon juice and Tabasco.

SERVE with a crusty loaf of sourdough bread.

Serves 4

Wine Suggestion: Serve with a chilled Oregon Pinot Gris.

Seared Pave of Salmon

with Potatoes, Peppers and Feta in Citrus Vinaigrette

Ingredients

- *4 portions of fresh salmon, pave cut*
- *1 pound red potatoes, ½" dice*
- *2 lemons*
- *1 tablespoon sugar*
- *½ cup extra virgin olive oil*
- *1 teaspoon dried oregano*
- *salt and pepper to taste*
- *1 red bell pepper, ¼" dice*
- *6 ounces feta cheese, crumbled*
- *1 head romaine lettuce*

Preparation

COOK the diced potatoes in some salted water until just cooked – but not mushy – 10 to 15 minutes. Remove from the heat and hold warm in their pot.

TO MAKE the vinaigrette, zest or grate the peel of the lemons and combine with the sugar and their juice in a small saucepan. Bring to a simmer and cook for 5-7 minutes. Remove from the heat and whisk in the olive oil, oregano, and season to taste with salt and pepper.

SEASON the salmon portions with salt and pepper. Heat a sauté pan with 2 tablespoons olive oil and when it just beings to smoke, sear the seasoned salmon portions in it – turning them when well browned – 3 to 4 minutes per side.

WHILE the salmon is cooking drain the remaining liquid from the warm potatoes and toss them with the diced pepper, crumbled feta and enough of the vinaigrette to moisten them well.

ARRANGE some romaine leaves on each plate, top with the potato salad mixture and then a portion of the cooked salmon – drizzle with more of the lemon vinaigrette if desired.

Serves 4

Wine Suggestion: Serve with a Brickhouse Pinot Noir.

Smoked Salmon and Onion Tart

Ingredients

- 1 pre-baked pie shell
- 1 stick unsalted butter
- 2 medium yellow onions, sliced
- 2 tablespoons flour
- ½ cup heavy cream
- 2 eggs
- 1 cup grated cheddar cheese
- 10 ounces smoked flaked salmon
- salt and pepper to taste

Preparation

MELT butter in sauté pan, add onions, and sweat without browning (medium heat) until soft and translucent.

TRANSFER to medium sized bowl and stir in flour, cream, and eggs; gently fold in cheese and salmon. Season to taste with salt and pepper.

POUR in pre-baked pie shell and bake at 350° until golden brown and set, approximately 45-60 minutes.

Serves 6-8

Wine Suggestion: Serve with a Chehalem Pinot Gris.

THE WINE SPECTATOR AWARD

Many of the restaurants included in this cookbook have been recognized by Wine Spectator, the world's most popular wine magazine. It reviews more than 10,000 wines each year and covers travel, fine dining and the lifestyle of wine for novices and connoisseurs alike. Through its Restaurant Awards program, the magazine recognizes restaurants around the world that offer distinguished wine lists.

Awards are given in three tiers. In 2003, more than 3,600 restaurants earned wine list awards. To qualify, wine lists must provide vintages and appellations for all selections. The overall presentation and appearance of the list are also important. Once past these initial requirements, lists are then judged for one of three awards: the Award of Excellence, the Best of Award of Excellence, and the Grand Award.

- Award of Excellence—The basic Award of Excellence recognizes restaurants with lists that offer a well-chosen selection of quality producers, along with a thematic match to the menu in both price and style.
- Best of Award of Excellence—The second-tier Best of Award of Excellence was created to give special recognition to those restaurants that exceed the requirements of the basic category. These lists must display vintage depth, including vertical offerings of several top wines, as well as excellent breadth from major wine growing regions.
- Grand Award—The highest award, the Grand Award, is given to those restaurants that show an uncompromising, passionate devotion to quality. These lists show serious depth of mature vintages, outstanding breadth in their vertical offerings, excellent harmony with the menu, and superior organization and presentation. In 2003, only 89 restaurants held Wine Spectator Grand Awards.

Jake's Famous Crawfish

401 SW 12th Ave.
Portland, OR 97205
503-226-1419
www.jakesfamouscrawfish.com

Monday -Thursday
11:00 am - midnight
Friday
11:00 am – 1:00 am
Saturday
Noon – 1:00 am
Sunday
3:00 pm - 11:00 pm

Jake's Famous Crawfish Restaurant

Tradition and great seafood are the two big drawing points for Jake's Famous Crawfish. Located at the corner of SW12th and Stark, this venerable restaurant has been serving mouth-watering food and fine drinks at this location since 1892. A colorful local character, Jacob (Jake) Freiman, established a Portland tradition when he served his first crawfish at the Oregon Hotel in 1881. He continued delighting Portland locals and visitors alike with his seafood dishes, and in 1920 he bought the fish house at the corner of SW 12th and Stark. In the 1970's, Bill McCormick and Doug Schmick, a duo who have become famous in their own right for Northwest seafood, purchased the restaurant and have kept the ambience that has been Jake's for all these years.

When entering the restaurant, you will feel the pull of the century-old surroundings. The original wooden booths are quite comfortable and give you extraordinary privacy. Many of the tables and sideboards are also original, and the walls are covered with a fascinating collection of 19th century oil paintings. The fantastic turn-of the-century bar is a fun place to have a pre-dinner libation. It has attracted many a Portland native, along with many celebrities who have stopped by when they have been in town; celebrities such as Sophie Tucker, Tommy Lee Jones, Jack Benny, Humphrey Bogart, and Paul Newman.

Tradition is great, but you can't eat it. However, Jake's Famous Crawfish lives up to the "famous" in its name. The large menu is printed daily and features over 30 varieties of fresh fish and seafood that is flown in, or obtained from local producers. The section of the menu devoted to oysters on the half shell usually has 8 or 9 species of oysters from the Northwest Coast and Canada. One of the signature dishes is Jake's Clam Chowder, a rich and creamy concoction that has an abundance of fresh clams in it. Jake's Etouffe is a wonderful rendition of an old Louisiana dish, rich with crawfish, chicken, and shrimp. If fresh wild salmon is your passion, you can get it smoked and served with a remoulade sauce as an appetizer, grilled simply with a sauce of the day, stuffed with Dungeness crab, bay shrimp and Brie cheese, or tossed with fettuccini and served with wild Oregon mushrooms sautéed with a Dijon cream sauce.

SEARED RARE AHI APPETIZER

Ingredients

4 3-ounce block cuts of ahi tuna (see note)
4 ounces daikon radish
4 ounces pickled ginger
4 ounces wasabi
4 ounces soy sauce
4 slices of fresh cucumber
Cajun Spice (recipe follows)

Preparation

DREDGE ahi in 3 teaspoons of the Cajun spice. In a hot pan, preferably cast iron, sear each side of the ahi for 10-15 seconds. This should give the ahi about ¼ inch border of doneness. Slice thinly, into about 5-7 pieces, about ¼-½ inches in size.

ARRANGE ahi on bed of shredded daikon and garnish with pickled ginger, wasabi, soy sauce, and piece of cucumber, thinly sliced lengthwise and rolled to resemble a rose.

NOTE: Buy sushi grade ahi tuna. Ask for it in block cuts.

For the Cajun Spice

3 tablespoons paprika
2 tablespoons salt
2 tablespoons garlic powder
1 teaspoon cayenne
1 teaspoon white pepper
1 teaspoon black pepper
1 teaspoon thyme
1 teaspoon oregano

MIX together well.

Serves 4

JAKE'S HOUSE SALAD

with Glazed Walnuts and Crumbled Bleu Cheese

Ingredients

8 ounces mesclun mix salad greens
8 ounces crumbled blue cheese
Glazed Walnuts (recipe follows)
Dressing (recipe follows)

Preparation

MAKE the glazed walnuts and the dressing. In large bowl combine salad and 2-3 ounces of the dressing and toss. Arrange on plate and top with blue cheese crumbles and glazed walnuts

For the Glazed Walnuts

2 cups walnuts
water to boil
1-1½ cups powder sugar
oil to fry

BOIL walnuts for about 2 minutes. Drain well. Mix with 1 to 1½ cups powdered sugar, coating well. In a deep pan, heat oil to approximately 350 degrees. Deep fry walnuts, being careful not to bunch them together. Cook until brown, turning as needed. Remove with slotted spoon to flat pan to cool.

Dressing

1 cup dark balsamic vinegar
1 cup olive oil
2 cups salad oil
1 teaspoon white pepper
1 teaspoon black pepper
1 tablespoon Dijon mustard
1 teaspoon salt
1 teaspoon chopped garlic
½ teaspoon sugar

PUT aside the oils. Blend all other ingredients well. While blending, slowly add the oils.

Serves 4

Crawfish and Chicken Etouffee

This signature dish is served at the table from a cast iron pot. World famous New Orleans Chef Paul Prudhomme gave this classic recipe his stamp of approval while visiting Jake's in the 1980s.

Ingredients

- *8 ounces chicken*
- *1 tablespoon olive oil*
- *8 ounces rock shrimp*
- *8 ounces crawfish tails*
- *Etouffee Base (recipe follows)*

Preparation

MAKE the etouffee base. Sauté chicken in olive oil until almost done. Add rock shrimp and sauté for approximately 2 minutes, then add crawfish tails and cook until heated throughout. Add 3 cups etouffee base and simmer. We suggest serving with white rice.

For the Etouffee Base

- *1 cup oil*
- *1½ cups flour*
- *1 teaspoon salt*
- *½ teaspoon pepper*
- *½ teaspoon dry thyme*
- *½ teaspoon paprika*
- *½ teaspoon basil*
- *¼ teaspoon white pepper*
- *½ teaspoon cayenne*
- *1 cup celery*
- *1½ cups onion*
- *¾ cup green pepper*
- *¼ cup red pepper*
- *6 cups water*
- *2 tablespoons fish bouillon powder*

HEAT oil in heavy pan until just below the smoking point. Add flour and stir constantly until mixture turns golden brown. Add all seasonings and cook on low heat for about 10 minutes. Add vegetables and cook another 5 minutes. Pour in water and fish bouillon and simmer for 15 minutes. When complete, this mixture should be velvet smooth and ready to use.

Serves 2

Wine Suggestion: Tyee Gewurtztramer

Crab and Shrimp Cakes

We use Dungeness crab, however blue crab or snow crab may be substituted.

Ingredients

- *1 pound crabmeat*
- *1½ pounds bay shrimp*
- *¾ cup celery, finely diced*
- *½ cup onion, finely diced*
- *1½ cups mayonnaise*
- *1 tablespoon Worcestershire sauce*
- *3 tablespoons Dijon mustard*
- *1 tablespoon lemon juice*
- *4 cups panko bread crumbs*
- *¼ teaspoon cayenne pepper*
- *½ teaspoon salt*
- *½ teaspoon white pepper*
- *1 teaspoon dry mustard*
- *1 egg*

Preparation

DRAIN crab and shrimp.

COMBINE celery and onion with mayonnaise, Worcestershire sauce, Dijon mustard and lemon juice. Mix well. Add crab and shrimp and half the panko crumbs. Gently mix together being careful not to break apart the crab legs. Form the mixture into a ball the size you want and form into a disc. An easy way to get a uniform size and shape is to use a small flat-bottomed bowl as a form. Combine the remaining panko bread crumbs, cayenne pepper, salt, white pepper and dry mustard in a shallow dish or pan. Whisk the egg in a bowl. Dip each crab cake in the egg mixture and gently press. Gently press the cake surface into the other half of the panko bread crumbs to coat. Pan fry over medium heat until brown on both sides.

Serves 4–6

Wine Suggestion: Willakenzie Estates Pinot Gris

Crab Leg Sauté

This is one of Jake's most popular entrees. The lure of eating a mountain of crab legs already out of the shell is often hard to resist.

Ingredients

5 ounces Dungeness crab legs
1 ounce drawn butter
3 ounces sliced mushrooms
½ teaspoon finely diced shallots
salt and pepper to taste
½ ounce sherry wine
sprinkle of chopped parsley
1 tablespoon whole butter
1 teaspoon lemon juice

Preparation

HEAT drawn butter in sauté pan until hot. Add mushrooms and sauté until about half cooked. Add shallots and salt and pepper to taste. Add crab legs and deglaze by adding a small amount of the sherry, then stirring to loosen browned bits of food from the pan. Simmer for about 30 seconds, then add in chopped parsley, whole butter and lemon juice.

Serves 1

Wine Suggestion: Cameron Chardonnay

Stuffed Salmon

Combining two of the Northwest's most popular seafoods, salmon and Dungeness crab, this dish receives rave reviews year after year.

Ingredients

1 5-ounce salmon fillet
2 ounces fish stock or 1 ounce white wine and 1 ounce water

Preparation

CUT pocket in salmon fillet by placing knife on the outer, upper edge, about ½ inch from top of fillet. Slice in about 2½ inches, and down about 3 inches.

MAKE the salmon stuffing. Fill pocket with stuffing and place in shallow pan with fish stock or water/wine mix. Place in 350 degree oven for about 14 minutes or until fully cooked. Should be slightly firm to the touch. Serve with favorite vegetables and potatoes.

For the Salmon Stuffing

1 ounce bay shrimp
½ ounce crabmeat
1½ ounce cream cheese
½ ounce Brie cheese
salt and pepper

MIX the shrimp, crabmeat, cream cheese, and Brie together well and then add salt and pepper to taste.

Serves 1

Wine Suggestion: Cristom Vineyards Pinot Noir

Jake's Three Berry Cobbler

Marionberries are a hybrid of blackberries. Blackberries may be used in areas where marionberries are not available.

Ingredients

3 pounds blueberries
3 pounds marionberries
3 pounds raspberries
4 tablespoons water
3 tablespoons sugar
4½ tablespoons cornstarch
2 tablespoons lemon juice
Crust (recipe follows)

Preparation

IN A stockpot mix together the water, sugar, cornstarch and lemon juice and bring just to a boil. Add the blueberries. Let it cook for about 12 – 15 minutes, stirring occasionally. It should start to look like jam. Remove it from the heat and add the remaining berries. Blend well.

SPOON one cup of the filling into cobbler bowls. Top with the crust and bake at 375 degrees for 12 – 15 minutes or until golden brown. While they are cooling, you can sprinkle some sugar over the crust.

For the Crust

2½ cups flour
1 tablespoon baking powder
2 tablespoons sugar
½ pound butter
2 eggs
⅔ cup milk

COMBINE flour, baking powder, and sugar and mix together well. Cut in the butter. Add in the eggs and milk. Stir until blended, but be careful not to over mix.

ON A floured cutting board, roll out the dough to ⅛th inch thickness. Cut into desired size.

Serves 6

W. Burnside at 3rd Avenue ca. 1915.

Mother's Bistro

409 SW Second Ave.
Portland, OR 97204
503-464-1122
www.mothersbistro.citysearch.com

Tuesday – Thursday
7:00 am – 10:00 pm
Friday
7:00 am – 11:00 pm
Saturday
9:00 am – 11:00 pm
Sunday
9:00 am – 2:30 pm

Mother's Bistro & Bar

Lisa Schroeder, the owner-chef of Mother's Bistro, has a philosophy that has helped her establish a unique restaurant in Portland. Her philosophy is based on the idea that "home-cooked food is the best food. I'm talking about the kind of foods our mothers or grandmothers used to make, slow-cooked foods that take hours to prepare: hand-made dumplings, stews, roasts and braised dishes." Lisa graduated from the prestigious Culinary Institute of America in New York. She furthered her education as an apprentice with French superstars Roger Verge and Mark Veyrat, and traveled all over Europe learning about regional cuisines.

Since opening Mother's in 2000, Lisa has featured dishes that are based on traditional slow-cooked recipes and classic techniques. Regular features on the menu are entrees such as slow-cooked chicken with herbed dumplings and flavorful stews like the Cioppino, full of seafood in a rich white wine and tomato broth. The "Painted Hills" (a local natural beef company) meatloaf is topped with crispy bacon and smothered with gravy and served with creamy, buttery smashed red potatoes. The menu includes a number of dishes that come from Lisa's own mother, Belle. Her chicken noodle soup is served daily as well as her mom's recipe for chopped liver, a chicken liver pate sweetened with slow-cooked onions. Lisa creates everything from scratch, including all stocks and sauces.

Mother's Bistro does not serve just American comfort foods. Her worldwide travels have confirmed her philosophy. Lisa believes that some of the best food is cooked in the home with recipes passed down from earlier generations. She has set up a unique concept. Each month the restaurant features a Mother of the Month, and serves the recipes created by that mother, sometimes with a little refinement. Lisa has featured mothers from Morocco, Hungary, Mexico, Austria, Italy and New York to name a few.

After you have had one of Lisa's great home-cooked meals, try to save room for one of her desserts. Pastry Chef, Debbie Putnam, has an impressive array of homemade pies, dark chocolate or caramel bread pudding and outstanding fruit crisps, which celebrate Oregon's local berry farms and orchards.

Mother's has received national acclaim in publications such as Food and Wine magazine, Bon Appetit, and Northwest Palate among others. Lisa has recently completed a cookbook that will be out in the near future.

MOTHER'S BUTTERMILK BISCUITS & COUNTRY GRAVY

Ingredients

- 1 *quart self-rising flour*
- ½ *tablespoon kosher salt*
- ¼ *cup sugar*
- 4 *ounces cold butter, cut into small cubes*
- 1¾ *cups buttermilk*
- 1½ *cups heavy cream*
- ½ *pound melted butter*
- *extra flour for dusting biscuits*
- *Gravy (recipe follows)*
- *Italian parsley for garnish*

Preparation

PREHEAT oven to 500 degrees.

PLACE flour, salt and sugar in a large mixing bowl. Using a pastry blender or whisk, cut butter into dry ingredients until the butter is the size of a pea. Add liquid and using your hands, stir just until incorporated. Do not over mix and don't worry, the batter will be wet.

PLACE about 3 cups of flour into another mixing bowl. Using an ice cream scoop, scoop a portion of the batter directly into the flour and toss lightly to coat. Remove and place on a rimmed cookie sheet or other baking pan with sides at least one inch high. Continue with the rest of the dough, placing the floured biscuits directly next to each other (they should be touching).

BAKE biscuits for 5 minutes. Turn oven down to 475 degrees and bake biscuits until very brown – about 15-20 minutes. Remove from oven and brush with melted butter.

TO SERVE, place biscuits on a serving plate. Top with gravy, sprinkle with chopped fresh Italian parsley and serve.

For Gravy

- 2½ *pounds good pork sausage, bulk (no casing)*
- 1½ *quarts heavy cream*
- 1½ *quarts whole milk*
- 1 *tablespoon granulated garlic*
- 1 *tablespoon granulated onion*
- 1 *tablespoon black pepper*
- ½ *tablespoon dry thyme*
- ½ *tablespoon cayenne pepper*
- ¾ *cup reserved sausage fat*
- 1 *cup all-purpose flour*
- *salt to taste*

IN A large but shallow pot (like a Dutch oven), sauté pork sausage until lightly browned, breaking it into small pieces.

MEANWHILE, in another pot, heat milk and cream and add seasonings.

Mother's Buttermilk Biscuits & Country Gravy

CONTINUED

STRAIN cooked sausage and save the fat. Pour reserved fat (you need ¾ cup – if you do not have it, add either bacon fat or butter to equal ¾ cup) back into the pot where you cooked the sausage. Add flour, mixing with a wooden spoon or whisk and cook a few minutes.
Add the hot milk mixture to the flour mixture (you are making a roux, which will thicken the gravy) in the pot and stir well to make sure there are no lumps, scraping up the bits of sausage from the bottom of the pot.

ONCE you are sure that your gravy is not lumpy, add sausage to hot milk mixture and continue to cook about half an hour, stirring frequently with a wooden spoon to be sure the bottom does not burn. Add salt to taste.

Makes 16 biscuits

Chicken & Dumplings & Chicken Soup

Ingredients

- *2 whole chickens and other carcasses, if available*
- *2 whole onions, peeled*
- *4 stalks celery*
- *4 whole carrots, peeled*
- *4 parsnips, peeled*
- *1 bunch flat leaf (Italian) parsley*
- *fresh cold water to cover*
- *salt and freshly ground pepper, to taste*
- *2 cups finely diced carrots*
- *2 cups finely diced celery*

Preparation

IN A big pot, put in the chickens, onion, celery, carrots, parsnips, and parsley. Cover with at least 1½ gallons of cold water. Bring to a boil and skim scum. Season lightly with salt and pepper.

SIMMER the broth, uncovered, for at least 3 hours. Lift the chicken from the pot and set aside until cool enough to handle. Strain the rest of the broth into a clean pot. Add the diced celery and carrots and cook until just tender.

WHILE the vegetables are cooking, pick through the chicken, trying to leave the pieces as large as possible, discarding the bones. Set aside.

COOK packaged egg noodles according to directions, strain, and run cold water over them to stop the cooking. Set aside.

TO SERVE soup, add some of the cooked, picked chicken back to soup pot (you can make chicken salad with the rest of the boiled chicken, or reserve it for Chicken and Dumplings, recipe below). Taste soup for seasoning. Place noodles in serving bowls. Ladle broth, chicken, and vegetables into bowls and enjoy.

For Chicken and Dumplings
Ingredients

- ½ *pound unsalted butter*
- ¾ *pound flour*
- 3 *cups flour*
- 1 *tablespoon baking powder*
- ½ *tablespoon salt*
- 2 *tablespoons finely chopped Italian parsley*
- 2 *tablespoons solid shortening (like Crisco) or butter*
- 1-1¼ *cups milk*
- *chicken broth (from soup, above)*
- *chicken (from recipe above)*

Preparation

WHILE the soup is cooking, make the roux by melting the butter over medium heat in a saucepan. Add the ¾ pound of flour and mix with a whisk to ensure that there are no lumps. Cook over medium heat while stirring for about 5 minutes, until the mixture resembles sand on the beach. It should not darken. Set aside.

WHEN ready, add the roux to the broth mixture and return to a boil while whisking to remove any lumps. Let cook for a bit to cook out the flour taste.

WHILE this is cooking, make the dumpling dough by combining the flour, baking powder, salt, and parsley in a bowl. Using a pastry blender or fork, cut in the shortening until the mixture resembles coarse meal. Add 1 cup of milk and stir briefly to blend. Add only enough of the remaining milk to make the dough hold together. Drop spoonfuls of dumpling dough into the rouxed broth. Cover and cook for 20 minutes (do not lift cover during cooking).

TO SERVE dumplings, place a piece of chicken in a serving bowl. Add dumplings and broth.
Sprinkle with fresh chopped parsley and serve.

Serves 10

Perfect Pot Roast

This is by far the most popular dish on our menu at Mother's Bistro & Bar. The main reason is probably because it is the one dish I always recommend to first-time visitors to Mother's. It typifies what we do best – slow-cooked food that takes hours to prepare, made with the best possible ingredients using classic cooking techniques. Mastering Pot Roast is the first step to understanding how to braise – an important cooking technique when preparing Mother Foods. There are similar steps in every braised dish – browning the meat, sautéing aromatic vegetables, adding a flavorful liquid – take a look at the notes for more braising tips. Pot Roast, like most braised dishes, freezes and reheats well, so if you want to have leftovers, just double or triple the recipe. Serve it with Perfect Smashed Potatoes – they are a great foil for rich, deep flavors of the savory Pot Roast gravy. Don't skimp on the meat – buy the best, most natural, freshest beef you can afford – the taste will be infinitely better.

Ingredients

- 4 *pounds beef chuck (sometimes referred to as chuck neck roll)*
- *salt and freshly ground black pepper to taste*
- ¼ *cup vegetable oil*
- 2 *onions, peeled and chopped*
- 2 *carrots, peeled and chopped*
- 2 *stalks celery, chopped*
- 3 *cloves garlic, peeled*
- ¾ *cup tomato puree*
- ¼ *cup all-purpose flour*
- 1 *cup red wine*
- 1 *bouquet garni (thyme, parsley sprigs, bay leaf)*
- 2½ *quarts beef or veal stock*

Preparation

PREHEAT oven to 350 degrees.

TRIM beef of excess fat and sinew and season very well with salt and pepper. Heat a Dutch oven or other large heavy casserole until very hot. Add oil, then beef, and sear until browned on all sides.

REMOVE beef and place it on a large plate. Don't worry about keeping it warm – you'll be putting it back into the pot to cook for many more hours. Add chopped onion, carrot, celery, and garlic (by the way, don't worry about chopping these vegetables too fine. They are going to cook for a few hours, so they can be cut into half inch pieces). Sauté over high heat until slightly browned, turn down heat to medium, and continue to cook the vegetables until they are very soft, about 7 minutes. Add the tomato puree and cook until slightly browned, about 5 minutes.

ADD flour, stir, and cook for 3-4 minutes. Add the wine and bouquet garni and stir well, scraping to release anything stuck to the bottom of the pan. Return the meat to the pan and add the stock little by little mixing well with a wooden spoon, adding only enough to cover up two-thirds of the meat. The amount of stock necessary varies and depends on what size and type of pot you are using. If too much stock is added, the final flavors of the dish will be diluted and less intense. Bring to a boil, cover with lid or aluminum foil and place in the oven until the beef is fork-tender, about two hours. I like to cook braised dishes and stews in the oven because it cooks more evenly. If you aren't blessed with the world's best pans, this ensures that you don't get any burned spots on your pan, and possible burned tastes in your food.

IF SERVING immediately, lift the beef out of the pot using tongs or a spatula and keep warm on a plate tented with foil. Strain the sauce through a sieve into another pot. Degrease the sauce by dragging a ladle over the top of the sauce to catch any fat that has risen and discard. Repeat until most of the fat is removed. If the sauce is too thin cook, over medium high heat, stirring occasionally, until slightly thicker. Adjust seasoning with salt and pepper.

SLICE beef and serve with the sauce. Don't worry about getting beautiful slices – chunks of this tender meat are fine and just as delicious.

IF MAKING this ahead of time, (it keeps well in the refrigerator for 3-4 days), remove the meat from pan and let cool. Strain the sauce into another container and refrigerate. Once cool, wrap the meat in plastic and refrigerate. One hour before serving, remove the sauce from the refrigerator, scrape off any fat that has congealed on the top, and discard. Slice the beef and put in an ovenproof serving dish, pour sauce over meat, cover, place in a 350 degree oven for 30-45 minutes and serve.

NOTES:

- Don't use a cut of meat that is too good for the job – braised dishes are meant to be made with less expensive cuts of meat. Cuts of meat such as chuck are tougher and fattier, but they only get better the longer they cook. When you use more expensive or less fatty cuts, they actually toughen with longer cooking times.
- Bouquet Garni is a French term that refers to herbs – parsley, thyme and bay leaf – used to flavor soups, stews, sauces, and other dishes. Many cookbooks call for the bouquet garni to be wrapped in cheesecloth, or tied together so they can be easily lifted out of the dish. When a sauce is going to be strained later (as with the Pot Roast), there is no need to go to the trouble of tying the herbs or wrapping in cheesecloth. Just toss the herbs into the pot for Pot Roast.
- If you are using homemade veal stock in this recipe, then season the meat generously with salt and freshly ground pepper, as called for in the recipe, since that is where the sauce and meat will be getting most of their flavor. If using canned beef broth, even low-sodium, season the meat only lightly with salt. The gravy will be getting most of its saltiness from the broth. Be sure, however, to taste the sauce toward the end of the cooking and adjust the seasonings

with salt and freshly ground black pepper as necessary. If you think the sauce is too thin, and needs to reduce slightly, do not season with salt until the very end, as the salt flavor will concentrate as the sauce reduces.

- It is important to choose the right pan for the job. It should have a bottom large enough for the meat to fit in one layer, but not so large that there are empty spots which might burn while the meat is searing. Also, if the pan is too big, you will need more stock to cover the meat, which will dilute the flavor of the final dish.
- Browning meat is a vital step in all braised dishes and stews. Contrary to popular belief, browning doesn't "lock in juices," but it does caramelize the outside of the meat which adds another layer of flavor to the final dish, making it that much more delicious. Notice that the recipe calls for heating the pan first, and then adding oil. This is a procedure followed in most professional kitchens – a pan used for sautéing or searing is heated before adding anything else. It allows the pan to get hot enough to sear or sauté without having the oil get smoky. If your pan is not hot enough, the natural moisture in the meat will cause it to boil and turn gray rather than browned and caramelized.
- The best way to tell when a braised item is cooked is by piercing it with a two-prong fork and trying to lift it out of the pan. If the meat falls back into the pot right away, it is done. If it comes up with the fork, it needs more time.

Serves 10

Pazzo Ristorante

627 SW Washington St.
Portland, OR 97205
503-228-1515
www.pazzoristorante.com

Monday - Friday
7:00 am - 10:00 pm
Saturday
8:00 am - 11:00 pm
Sunday
8:00 am - 10:00 pm

Pazzo Ristorante

Pazzo Building

The Pazzo Ristorante is located in downtown Portland, in the historic Hotel Vintage Plaza. The building first opened its doors in March of 1894 to the accolades of the Oregonian, who declared, the "...opening of the hotel...was an event of considerable importance in the history of the city of Portland."

F. Manson White, a prominent local architect, designed a strong, solid, and impressive building, one of the first in the Romanesque-style in the Pacific Northwest. The stone and brick made the hotel nearly fireproof, and the lobby had oak paneling, leather upholstery, and elegant Brussels carpeting. At the turn of the century, clientele included industrialists, merchants, bankers, railway executives, and theatrical people, and it was an active center for state politics.

Today Pazzo is popular with visitors and residents alike. The wood-burning pizza stove and exhibition kitchen are welcoming and the delicious aroma of Italian cooking whets the appetite. Here you will find the elegant old world charm of Northern Italy in the heart of downtown Portland.

Noteworthy cocktails include the classic Martini, Manhattan, and Pazzo's very own Lemon Drop and Mocha Bianca. The selection of scotch and bourbon is a distinguished collection of single-malt scotch and single-barrel bourbons, and the cognac, armagnac, brandy, ports and grappe are excellent.

Pazzo is conveniently located two blocks from Pioneer Square, within easy walking distance of shopping and theaters, and a wonderful place to spend that special evening.

Tonno Marinata

Ingredients

- 14 ounces best quality Yellowfin Tuna, diced in ¼" cubes
- 5 tablespoons olive oil
- ½ tablespoon ground Japanese pepper threads
- salt and pepper to taste
- 2 oranges, filets in juice
- 1 treviso or ¼ radicchio, shredded
- 8 large basil leaves, chiffonade

Preparation

BLEND the olive oil and the pepper threads in a small blender. Set aside.

PLACE the tuna in a mixing bowl, and season lightly with salt and pepper. Add oranges, treviso (or radicchio), and basil, and mix well. Taste for seasoning, and portion the mixture onto 4 plates, leaving the orange juice in the bowl.

TO SERVE, drizzle the olive oil mixture on top and some on the side.

Serves 4

Wild Oregon Salmon

with Favetta and Lemon- Balsamic Vinaigrette

Ingredients

- 4 *6-ounce filets wild Oregon salmon, skin on*
- 2½ *cups fresh fava beans, blanched and shelled*
- 4 *sprigs fresh thyme, leaves only, chopped*
- 1 *cup extra virgin olive oil*
- ¼ *cup water*
- *salt to taste*
- 3 *teaspoons balsamic vinegar*
- 1 *drop lemon oil*
- 1 *endive, core removed, sliced into long julienne slices*
- ½ *lemon*

Preparation

IN A food processor, finely chop the fava beans with thyme, ½ cup of the olive oil and water to just rotate the contents. Blend favas until somewhat smooth and season with salt.

GRILL salmon filets to desired temperature. In the meantime, pour the balsamic vinegar, lemon oil, and the remaining olive oil in a bowl. Set this vinaigrette aside.

HEAT the favetta on medium heat, stirring often. Place the puree on the center of the plate, spoon vinaigrette around it, and place salmon on top. Place the endive in a small bowl and season with salt, pepper, and juice from the half lemon. Set some endive on the salmon and serve.

Pazzo dining room.

Panna Cotta di Canela
Cinnamon Panna Cotta

Ingredients

5 *teaspoons powdered gelatin, unflavored*
5 *tablespoons cold water*
1 *cup whole milk*
2 *ounces sugar*
2 *cups cream*
1 *cinnamon stick, crushed*
Rhubarb Compote (recipe follows)

Preparation

MAKE rhubarb compote. For the panna cotta. whisk gelatin and water together a bowl. Let the gelatin dissolve for at least five minutes.

IN A high-sided pot, bring milk, sugar, cream and cinnamon stick to a simmer. Take off the heat, and let the cinnamon infuse for five minutes. Add the two mixtures. Strain the mixture through a fine mesh sieve. Pour into 4-ounce ramekins, and let chill in the refrigerator for at least five hours. To serve, top with rhubarb compote.

For the Rhubarb Compote

¾ *cup white wine*
¾ *cup sugar*
¼ *teaspoon vanilla bean paste*
2 *ripe stalks of rhubarb, washed and diced*

IN A saucepan, bring wine and sugar up to a boil. Turn heat down to medium and add vanilla paste and rhubarb. Cook the mixture until the rhubarb has started to break down and release its own juice. Transfer to a wide bowl and cool immediately.

Serves 6

Black Plums Marinated in Honey and Fennel Pollen

Ingredients

5 ripe black plums, sliced in ½" wide wedges
3 tablespoons wildflower honey, a touch more if desired
a pinch fennel pollen, Tuscan variety
2 tablespoons dry white wine

Preparation

COMBINE everything in a bowl. Mix well, and let marinate for 2 ½ hours. Chill well and serve.

Serves 2

Wine celler.

214 SW Broadway
Portland, OR 97205
503-241-3393
www.saucebox.com

Tuesday – Thursday
4:30 pm – midnight
Friday
4:30 pm – 2:30 am
Saturday
5:00 pm – 2:30 am

Saucebox

Open since 1995, Saucebox was named "Restaurant of the Year" in 1998 by The Oregonian. It has also been featured in the New York Times, Bon Appetit, and Travel & Leisure. The Saucebox pioneered the Portland DJ-Café movement offering a luxurious downtown dinner experience that transforms itself into a hip live DJ scene at 10 p.m.

Enter through the beautiful carved wood and glass doors that support a lovely arched transom filled with beveled glass. The interior of the restaurant features a large mural by local celebrated artist Daniel Duford, and the dining room provides a venue for huge-scale art pieces that challenge the common aesthetic for restaurants everywhere.

The original owners, Bruce Carey and Christopher Israel had collaborated first on Zefiro Restaurant in 1990. They then opened Saucebox, putting an equal emphasis on fine food, fine service, and a distinctive vibe. When Chris left Oregon to take a position at Vanity Fair Magazine in New York, he sold his shares to Joe Rogers, who now partners with Bruce in keeping the restaurant fresh and stimulating.

Saucebox is known for its specialty cocktails, including seasonally changing fruit infusions. These cocktails complement a menu featuring Hawaiian and Pan Asian cuisine. Chef Adam Kekahuna has created a fantastic selection featuring the freshest ingredients that are native to these two regions. Chef Adam is a native Polynesian who graduated from Portland's Western Culinary Institute. He returned to Hawaii after his education in order to reaffirm his love of his native cooking. His creations at Saucebox are unique in their combination of these two cuisines. His signature dish, Javanese Roasted Salmon served with a sauce of soy, hot pepper, garlic, palm sugar and lime, was quoted by the New York Times as "quite possibly the best salmon ever!" But, there are many other tempting items on his menu. Try the Clay Pot Pork, a combination of marinated pork braised in a Vietnamese caramel sauce with fresh chives, scallions, and cilantro. The appetizers are exceptional, with several renditions of spring rolls, and the salads are unusual combinations such as the Banana Blossom Salad, with poached shrimp, roasted peanuts, onion, cilantro, and fried rice crackers.

Sweet Potato Spring Rolls

with Sour Lime Dipping Sauce

These make a delicious snack and always a welcome appetizer. Before frying the rolls, be sure they are completely dried or the excess moisture will cause them to burst open in the oil. Dip the rolls in the Sour Lime sauce and eat them while they're hot and crunchy.

Ingredients

- 1-2 *medium-sized sweet potatoes such as Garnet or Jewel, peeled and cut into julienne to equal 1 cup*
- 1-2 *medium-sized Boniato sweet potatoes, peeled and cut into julienne to equal 1 cup*
- ¼ *cup kosher salt*
- 2 *ounces mung bean thread noodles*
- ½ *cup (1½ ounces) dried tree ear mushrooms or dried black trumpet mushrooms*
- 2 *tablespoons vegetable or peanut oil*
- 8 *ounces bean sprouts*
- 2 *tablespoons grated or finely chopped palm sugar or brown sugar*
- 2 *tablespoons unseasoned rice wine vinegar*
- ½ *cup shredded Napa cabbage*
- ½ *teaspoon kosher salt and a few grindings of fresh black pepper*
- 12-14 *8-inch square spring roll wrappers (There are usually 25 sheets to one 12 ounce package), defrosted if frozen*
- 1 *egg, lightly beaten, for brushing the wrappers*
- 4-6 *cups peanut or vegetable oil, for frying*
- 1 *small head red or green lettuce, for serving*
- 1 *cup coarsely chopped cilantro*
- ¼ *cup mint, coarsely chopped*
- *Sour Lime Dipping Sauce (recipe follows)*

Preparation

IN A large bowl, combine both types of sweet potatoes and the salt and toss together. Transfer to a large strainer to drain and place 2-3 small plates on top to help push out the liquid. Let stand for about an hour. Using your hands, squeeze the excess liquid out of the vegetables. To remove the salt, rinse several times under cool water, tossing with your hands. Drain well, press out the liquid with your hands again, and lay out on a kitchen towel to dry for about 30 minutes.

SOAK the bean thread noodles in hot tap water for about 35 minutes and drain well. Place the dried mushrooms in a bowl and pour over 1 cup boiling water. Allow to hydrate for about 25 minutes. Drain well and cut into julienne to equal 1½ cups.

HEAT a tablespoon of oil in a large, 12-inch sauté pan, and fry the bean sprouts for a minute over medium heat. Add the palm sugar and cook until melted and bubbling, about 3-4 minutes. Add the sweet potatoes and cook over medium heat until softened, about 7-8 minutes, stirring often so they don't stick to the pan and burn. Stir in the vinegar and cook

Sweet Potato Spring Rolls

with Sour Lime Dipping Sauce

CONTINUED

to reduce completely, about 3-5 minutes. Strain the mixture in a colander and spread it onto a baking sheet to dry out.

WIPE the skillet out and heat a teaspoon of oil over medium heat. Add the cabbage, salt, and pepper and cook 7 minutes, until soft and all of the liquid has evaporated. Transfer to a large bowl and combine with the sweet potato mixture, mushrooms, and noodles. Spread the entire mixture onto two baking sheets and cover with towels for about 30 minutes, until cool and dry. (The mixture must be completely cool before you stuff the wrappers or they will burst when frying.)

PLACE a wrapper on the work surface so it's in the shape of a diamond, with one of the corners pointing towards you. Spoon a heaping tablespoon of filling about 1½ inches in from the lower corner and fold the lower corner over the filling, gently pulling it towards you as you tuck it under the filling slightly. Lightly brush the two sides and the upper corner with egg wash. Bring the left and right corners over the filling to meet in the middle and roll it up tightly to seal. Place seam side down on parchment paper and allow to dry for 15 minutes before frying.

TO FRY, heat the oil in a medium sized, deep, heavy pot over medium heat until it reaches 350 degrees on a deep-fat thermometer, about 5 minutes. If you don't own a thermometer, you'll need to test a spring roll. The oil should bubble up immediately when you drop in the roll. If it doesn't, allow the oil to get a little bit hotter. Fry a few rolls at a time, about 3-4 minutes until golden brown, turning once with tongs to brown all sides. (Be careful not to crowd the rolls in the oil.) Drain on paper towels. Before adding the next batch of rolls, allow the oil to come back up to 350 degrees.

SERVE with the lettuce leaves piled next to the dipping sauce on a large platter. Use a lettuce leaf to pick up a roll and place a pinch of cilantro and mint in the leaf. Roll it around the spring roll and dip each bite in the sour lime dipping sauce.

For the Sour Lime Dipping Sauce

1 red Fresno chile or jalapeno, most of the seeds removed and finely chopped
¼ cup granulated sugar
4 limes
¼ cup fish sauce, such as 3 Crabs brand

USING a mortar and pestle, grind the chile and sugar into a coarse paste. Cut off both ends of the limes. Place one of the limes with the cut side down on a cutting board and slice off the peel, from top to bottom, following the contour of the fruit, removing as much of the white cottony pith as possible. Continue all the way around the fruit. Holding the lime in your hand or on a cutting board, carefully slice between the membrane and fruit to release the lime segments in between. Remove any seeds left in the segments.

ADD the lime sections and juice to the mortar and grind gently to make a pulpy and slightly chunky consistency. The fruit should be incorporated but not completely pulverized. Add the fish sauce and mix well. This will keep 5 days in the refrigerator.

Makes 12 rolls

Javanese Roasted Salmon

with Crispy Fried Leeks

The New York Times called this "quite possibly the best salmon ever!" This recipe, created by Saucebox founder Chef Christopher Israel, has been on the Saucebox menu for nearly nine years and customers insist it remain.

Ingredients

- 8 *six ounce salmon filets, preferably wild, skin removed*
- *kosher salt and freshly ground black pepper*
- 3 *tablespoons vegetable oil*
- 2 *large bunches spinach, stems removed, washed twice to remove all sand*
- *Sauce (recipe follows)*
- *Fried Leeks (recipe follows)*

Preparation

PREHEAT the oven to 375 degrees. Season the salmon filets on both sides with salt and pepper. Place a tablespoon or so of vegetable oil in a large, heavy-duty cast iron skillet and heat until very hot, over medium high heat, about 3-4 minutes. Place half of the filets in the hot skillet and sear until golden brown, about 3 minutes on each side. Transfer to a baking sheet or baking dish. Add a little more oil to the pan and sear the remaining filets in the same manner. Roast the salmon in the oven for 5-7 minutes, until medium rare to medium in the center.

MAKE the fried leeks and sauce. While the salmon is roasting, heat a tablespoon of oil in a large sauté pan over medium high heat and add about ¼ of the spinach leaves. Stir the spinach, allowing it to wilt before adding another batch. Stir constantly, until all of the spinach is wilted and tender. Place a few tablespoons of the cooked spinach in the center of each plate and arrange the salmon filets over it. Pour the warm sauce over the fish and spinach and garnish with the fried leeks on top.

Javanese Roasted Salmon
with Crispy Fried Leeks

CONTINUED

For the Fried Leeks

- *2 leeks, root end removed*
- *1½ cups peanut or vegetable oil, for frying*

CUT the tops off the leeks, leaving about one third of the green portion. Using a sharp knife, cut the leeks crosswise into 3 inch lengths. Slice the leeks into very thin strips or a fine julienne, about 1⁄16th of an inch thick. Rinse the leeks under cool running water for a few minutes to remove all of the sand. Spread them out on a towel and pat dry with another towel.

HEAT the oil in a small, deep, heavy-bottomed saucepan over medium heat to about 350 degrees. Be sure the leeks are very dry before frying them. Place about half the leeks in the oil and fry until they just begin to turn golden in color, about 1 minute. Transfer to a paper towel to drain and fry the remaining leeks in the same manner.

For the Sauce

- *1 stick (4 ounces) unsalted butter*
- *1 tablespoon dried red pepper flakes*
- *1 tablespoon finely chopped garlic*
- *½ cup grated or finely chopped palm sugar or brown sugar*
- *½ cup lime juice*
- *½ cup soy sauce, preferably Kecap Manis, the Indonesian variety*

MELT the butter in a small, heavy saucepan over medium heat. Add the chile flakes and garlic and stir until garlic starts to release its aroma, about 30 seconds, no longer (it shouldn't brown). Add the sugar to the mixture and whisk until it's dissolved and incorporated. Cook over medium heat about 3 minutes, until it starts bubbling on the surface. Add the lime juice and soy and return to a boil. Turn down the heat to low and simmer for about 2 minutes. Remove from the heat and re-warm once the salmon has finished cooking.

Makes 8 servings

Spicy Korean Baby Back Ribs

You know the ribs are done cooking when the bones become exposed on the ends and the meat is so tender you can push it off with a chopstick. Served with a cooling Cucumber Salad, this hearty dish is a crowd pleaser and easy to prepare.

Ingredients

1 cup soy sauce
½ cup sesame oil
½ cup brown sugar
4 scallions, white section and ⅓ of the green only, roughly chopped
½ cup chile-garlic sauce, (preferably Tuoung Ot toi Viet-nam brand)
2 tablespoons ginger, peeled and grated
5 pounds pork spareribs or 5 full 1 pound racks, cut into individual bones
Marinated Cucumber Salad (recipe follows)

Preparation

MAKE the marinade by combining the soy sauce, sesame oil, sugar, scallions, chile-garlic sauce, and ginger in a large bowl. Toss in the meat and marinate for at least 30 minutes, but preferably 2 hours. Transfer to a large roasting pan.

PREHEAT the oven to 400 degrees. Cover the roasting pan tightly with foil and bake the ribs for 1 hour. Remove the foil, being careful not to burn yourself when the steam escapes. Toss the ribs to coat well, replace the foil and seal. Bake for another 45 minutes or more until the meat is nearly falling off the bone and very tender.

NOTE: If you don't plan to eat the ribs right away, take them out of the sauce and chill the ribs and sauce separately. To reheat, allow the ribs and sauce to come to room temperature and warm them together in a 350 degree oven for 12-15 minutes. (Do not reduce while reheating or the sauce will become salty.)

TO SERVE, pile seven ribs on top of each other to form a tall stack or pyramid like shape. Serve with the marinated cucumber salad.

For the Marinated Cucumber Salad

¾ cup rice wine vinegar
¾ cup granulated sugar
2 English or Japanese cucumbers, halved and seeded
1 Thai chile, minced
1 tablespoon grated fresh ginger
1 shallot, peeled and thinly sliced

IN A small saucepan, heat the vinegar and sugar a minute or two until the sugar is dissolved. Allow to cool completely. Using a Japanese mandolin or a very sharp knife, slice the cucumbers thinly on the bias. Add the cucumber, chile, ginger, and shallot to the vinegar and marinate in the refrigerator for at least 3 hours. Remove from the refrigerator 30 minutes before serving.

Serves 8

Tapioca Dumplings

This Thai recipe was discovered by past Saucebox Chef Jon Beeaker while on sabbatical in Southeast Asia. They're fun to make and the components can be prepared in advance. Tapioca dumplings don't tolerate too much time out of the steamer so serve them immediately.

Ingredients

- 4 *cups small tapioca pearls, uncooked*
- 2 *tablespoons kosher salt*
- ¼ *cup tapioca flour or all-purpose flour*
- 4 *cups boiling water*
- 1½ *teaspoons coriander seeds*
- 1½ *teaspoons whole black peppercorns*
- 10 *garlic cloves, peeled and finely chopped*
- 6-8 *shallots, peeled and finely chopped to equal 1 cup*
- 1 *tablespoon peanut oil or vegetable oil*
- 1 *pound freshly ground chicken, uncooked*
- 1 *bunch cilantro, stems removed and coarsely chopped*
- ¼ *cup grated or finely chopped palm sugar*
- 6 *tablespoons fish sauce*
- ¾ *cup finely chopped peanuts*
- 6-8 *pieces of banana leaves or a few small sheets of parchment paper, for lining the steam basket (available fresh or frozen in Asian markets)*

Preparation

TO MAKE the dough, take a large bowl, and combine the tapioca pearls, salt, and flour. Pour the boiling water over the mixture and stir until just combined. Do not over stir or the mixture will become too pasty. The tapioca pearls should remain intact and moistened by the water, not dissolved. Transfer immediately onto a flat surface or two large baking sheets and spread out to cool.

MEANWHILE, make the filling. Toast the coriander and pepper in a small skillet over medium heat for 2-3 minutes, just until the spices release their aroma. When they're cool, grind them using a mortar and pestle or spice grinder until finely ground. Add the garlic, shallots, coriander, and peppercorns to the mortar and grind until a coarse paste or combine in a food processor.

IN A large sauté pan over medium high heat, warm the peanut oil and sauté the shallot-spice mixture about a minute until the aroma is released, stirring constantly. Add the ground chicken, stirring frequently. Cook about 5 minutes and add the cilantro, palm sugar, and fish sauce. Cook until the liquid is reduced and the chicken is cooked all the way through, about 3-5 minutes. Stir in the peanuts and set aside to cool.

TO FORM the dumplings, place a bowl of cool water next to your work area for dipping hands while forming the dumplings. Pinch off some dough (your hands should be slightly wet so that the dough doesn't stick, but not so wet that the pearls separate) about the size of a ping-pong ball and roll it between your palms to form a ball. Flatten the ball to about ¼ inch thick and place about a tablespoon of filling in the center of the dough, curling your palm around it so it folds up and forms sides. Pinch the sides together at the top to enclose it and roll it on your palm until it becomes a ball. Place the dumpling on a damp towel, and continue shaping the rest of the dumplings.

YOU must steam the dumplings in batches, in one layer, or they will stick to one another. To steam, line the steamer basket with a layer of banana leaf sections or parchment paper to prevent the dumplings from sticking. Bring the water in the steamer to a boil over high heat. Place one layer of dumplings on top of the leaf sections in the steamer, cover, and allow to steam for 8-10 minutes. Have an ice bath next to the steamer to keep your fingers from burning. You will need to use your hands to pluck each dumpling out, dipping your fingers in the ice bath before and after you remove each one. (The tapioca wrappers will stick to tongs, so don't even try.) Place the cooked dumplings on a banana leaf-lined platter and serve immediately. (The dumplings should be eaten right away or they'll dry out and lose their soft and sensual texture.) Check the water level under the steamer and add more if necessary to steam the next batch in the same manner.

Makes 36 dumplings

Tapioca Dumplings

Crispy Rice Pudding Spring Rolls

with Spicy Chocolate Sauce

This signature dessert was created by pastry chef Melissa McKinney.

Ingredients

- ½ *pound Arborio rice, rinsed until water runs clear*
- 1 *quart whole milk*
- 4 *cups coconut milk*
- ½ *vanilla bean, split and scraped*
- *zest of 1 lemon*
- ½ *teaspoon kosher salt*
- ½ *pound granulated sugar*
- 1 *package spring roll wrappers*
- *vegetable oil, for frying*
- *confectioner's sugar for dusting*
- *Spicy Chocolate Sauce (recipe follows)*

Preparation

IN A medium-sized, heavy-duty saucepan, combine the rice, milk, coconut milk, vanilla bean and scrapings, zest, salt, and sugar. Slowly bring to a boil, stirring constantly, and cook about 20 minutes, until the rice grains are al dente, and most of the liquid has been absorbed. Set aside and cool completely.

TO FORM the rolls, place a wrapper on the work surface so it's in the shape of a diamond, with one of the corners pointing towards you. Spoon a heaping tablespoon of filling about 1 ½ inches in from the lower corner and fold the lower corner over the filling, gently pulling it towards you as you tuck it under the filling slightly. Lightly brush the two sides and the upper corner with egg wash. Bring the left and right corners over the filling to meet in the middle and roll it up tightly to seal. Place seam side down on parchment paper. Continue with the remaining filling and wrappers.

IN A deep, heavy-bottomed saucepan, heat the oil to 350 degrees over medium heat. When the oil is hot, carefully place a few rolls into the oil and fry 2-3 minutes, turning them to brown completely. (Be careful not to crowd the pan.) When golden brown, remove from the oil onto paper towels to drain. Cool about 30 seconds. Slice diagonally through the center, sprinkle with confectioner's sugar and serve immediately with warm chocolate dipping sauce.

For the Spicy Chocolate Sauce

- 1 *cup whole milk*
- ½ *vanilla bean, split and scraped*
- *pinch of salt*
- 12 *ounces bittersweet chocolate, chopped into small pieces*
- 1½ *sticks unsalted butter, cut into small chunks*
- 1 *small jalapeno*
- 2 *tablespoons fresh orange juice*
- 1 *tablespoon Grand Marnier*

IN A small saucepan, combine the milk, vanilla bean and scrapings, and salt. Bring just to a boil over medium high heat and immediately turn off the heat. Allow to steep for 15 minutes. Place the chocolate, butter, and jalapeno pepper in a large bowl and pour the warm vanilla milk over it, stirring until all of the chocolate is melted. Add the orange juice and Grand Marnier and allow to sit for 20 minutes. Strain and when ready to serve, reheat over a double boiler until hot to the touch. (This can be made a few days ahead, brought to room temperature, and reheated before serving.)

Serves 8

Crispy Rice Pudding Spring Rolls

Downtown Portland ca.1877-1878.

Southpark Seafood Grill & Wine Bar

Located at the corner of S.W. 9th and Salmon Streets, Southpark is not only a great place to spend an evening enjoying a culinary treat, but also the perfect spot for before or after attending one of the many cultural performances in the area. Conveniently near the hub of the downtown Cultural District, Southpark is within walking distance to the Portland Center for the Performing Arts, the Arlene Schnitzer Concert Hall, the Oregon Historical Museum, and the Portland Art Museum to name a few.

The lively wine bar also serves small plates of many of their featured dishes, similar to the Spanish tapas tradition. The extensive wine list is set up in an unusual but creative manner. Instead of being listed according to geographical or varietal categories, Southpark has categorized their wines around stylistic groupings. For example, white wines are grouped into categories such as: "European style with minerality and finesse", "Modern New World style, rounded with rich fruit". The philosophy is to encourage guests to order by taste rather than by a familiar label, brand, or wine score. Encouraging experimentation, Southpark offers over 30 wines by the half glass as well as by the glass or carafe. They also offer a variety of wine flights that change regularly, as well as a daily wine and cheese pairing.

In the main dining room, seating is offered in a convivial atmosphere with comfy fabric-covered booths, beautifully restored wood floors, textured wall treatments, colorful artwork, and decorative iron railings and accents. Outside seating under large buttery yellow umbrellas is also available in the summer and early fall. The Mediterranean region heavily inspires Chef Ronnie MacQuarrie's menu. She expertly weaves the deliciously fresh northwest seafood and the finest imported specialty foods into her dishes. The Mediterranean influence can be seen in such luscious appetizers as the Moroccan Spiced Crab Cakes with mint, cilantro, and lime, or the Warm Dates stuffed with marcona almonds wrapped in jamon serrano. For entrees, try the classic Paella Valenciana with prawns, clams, mussels, chicken, and chorizo or the Catalan Seafood Stew with shrimp, scallops, mussels, clams, and romesco sauce. The dessert menu is delightful, with such specialties as Southpark Cannoli Towers, a scrumptious concoction of creamy ricotta and mascarpone filling studded with candied mandarin and semisweet chocolate chips wrapped in crispy vanilla cookie towers. Or, try the Summer Fruit Bread Pudding, featuring a house made brioche toasted and soaked in a gingered summer fruit compote and served chilled with vanilla bean mascarpone cream. Can't make up your mind? Not to worry, just order the Southpark Dessert Heaven, a sampler of both of these desserts along with a sample of the delicious Southpark Vanilla Bean Crème Brulee; enough to share with one or two friends.

Clams Cataplana

appetizer

Ingredients

- 30 *manila clams*
- 1 *pound pork tenderloin, diced in ¼ inch cubes*
- 1 *pound Portuguese chorizo sausage, sliced thinly*
- 2 *cloves minced garlic*
- 1 *large onion, small dice*
- ¼ *cup olive oil*
- 1 *roasted red pepper, peeled, seeded and cut into thin strips*
- 1 *yellow pepper, peeled, seeded and cut into thin strips*
- 2 *arbol chilies*
- 1 *bay leaf*
- ¼ *pound serrano ham, sliced thinly and cut in thin strips*
- 2 *28-ounce cans of good pear tomatoes*
- 1 *teaspoon Spanish smoked paprika*
- *salt and black pepper to taste*

Preparation

SAUTÉ the pork, sausage, garlic, and onion in the olive oil until the garlic starts to color. Add the peppers, chilies, bay leaf, and serrano ham and cook for about two minutes. Add the tomatoes and smoked paprika to the pan and let simmer for 10-15 minutes. Taste and adjust seasoning with salt and pepper.

Serves 4-6

Clams Cataplana

Southpark Mussels

appetizer

Ingredients

- *3 pounds black mussels*
- *2 tablespoons extra virgin olive oil*
- *½ pound Italian sausage*
- *1 tablespoon garlic*
- *½ cup Sambuca*
- *3 cups tomato sauce*
- *½ tablespoon chili flakes*
- *1 tablespoon orange zest*
- *salt and pepper to taste*

Preparation

RINSE the mussels in cold water then remove the beards from each. You should not use any mussels that are open and do not close when tapped. Put a small amount of oil in a pan and bring to a medium high heat. Add sausage, garlic, and mussels to the pan, cook until the garlic begins to color (stirring all the while). Add the Sambuca and let reduce almost all the way. Then add the tomato sauce, chili flakes, zest, salt, and pepper. Continue cooking until all of the mussels have opened. Three to four minutes should be enough. If some of the mussels do not open, discard them.

SERVE with a loaf of crusty bread.

Serves 6

Gazpacho

Ingredients

- 5 *pounds ripe tomatoes*
- *water to cook, salted*
- 2 *cups toasted bread crumbs*
- ½ *cup garlic*
- 2 *cups extra virgin olive oil*
- ¼ *cup sherry vinegar*
- *Salt and pepper to taste*
- *hard boiled egg, grated*
- *extra virgin olive oil, for garnish*
- *jamon serrano, julienne*

Preparation

BEGIN by cutting an x on the bottoms of the tomatoes. While doing this, bring one gallon water to a boil with a little salt. Place the tomatoes in the water and let boil until the skins begin to come loose. Remove from the water and place them in an ice bath to stop the cooking. Remove from the water and remove any skins that remain. Blend the tomatoes with the remaining ingredients until smooth. Garnish with grated hard-boiled eggs, extra virgin olive oil, and thinly sliced jamon serrano.

Serves 4

Gazpacho

Paella Valencia

Ingredients

- 1 *pound paella rice*
- ½ *medium yellow onion, diced small*
- 1½ *quarts chicken stock or water*
- ½ *tablespoon saffron, chopped*
- 1 *tablespoon Spanish paprika*
- 3 *prawns, peeled completely*
- ½ *pound chorizo sausage*
- 8 *ounces diced chicken*
- 1 *green bell pepper, diced small*
- 1 *red bell pepper, diced small*
- 12 *clams*
- 12 *mussels*
- *salt and pepper to taste*
- 2 *tablespoons butter*
- *chopped cilantro for garnish*

Preparation

IN A large sauté pan with a little olive oil sauté the onions until clear. Add the rice and cook until the rice is coated with the oil. Add all of the stock to the pan and bring to a boil. Once it begins boiling turn down the heat so it is at a simmer. Add the saffron and Spanish paprika to the rice. Stir the paella rice frequently. In a separate pan with a small amount of olive oil place the prawns, sausage, and chicken and sauté until slightly brown, then add the peppers, clams, and mussels. Let cook until the clams and mussels begin to open. Combine the rice with the shellfish and chicken and stir until the mixture begins to thicken. Continue stirring until the rice is tender. Remove the paella from the heat and stir in the butter. Serve with a sprinkle of chopped cilantro.

Serves 4

Wine suggestion : Chenin Blanc – Southpark recommends Domaine de la Sansonnière, La Lune, Anjou Blanc, France 2001 or an Albariño from Spain like Quinta de Couselo, O Rosal, Rias Baixas, Spain 2002

Chocolate Hazelnut Crostata

Ingredients

- 2 *cups sifted all purpose flour*
- 3 *tablespoons sugar*
- *pinch of salt*
- ¾ *cup chilled unsalted butter, cut into ¼ inch chunks*
- 2 *large egg yolks*
- 2 *tablespoons cold water*
- ½ *cup rough chopped toasted hazelnuts*
- *Crostata Filling (recipe follows)*
- *banana or vanilla ice cream (optional)*
- *powdered sugar for dusting*

Preparation

FOR pate sucre, take a medium bowl, and stir together flour, sugar, and salt. Add butter and rub between fingers with flour mixture until it resembles a coarse meal texture. Lightly whisk together yolks and water, add to flour mixture and stir with a fork until it comes together. Place on a floured surface and roll into a 3-inch wide log. Cover in plastic and refrigerate for ½ hour.

PREHEAT oven to 350 . Remove pate sucre from refrigerator. Divide into 6 equal portions. On a lightly floured surface, roll each portion into 8-inch diameter rounds. Sprinkle chopped hazelnuts onto the center of each round. Add a scoop of filling to the center of each, dividing evenly among the rounds. Slightly wet your hands and lightly flatten each portion of filling. Fold dough into center over filling, making 6 pleats in each crostata. Bake on a parchment lined cookie sheet until golden brown, about 15-20 minutes. Serve warm with banana or vanilla ice cream and dusted with powdered sugar.

For the Crostata Filling

- 12 *ounces Gianduia (hazelnut chocolate), chopped*
- ¾ *cup cream*
- ¼ *cup sugar*
- 6 *large egg yolks*

IN A medium saucepan, heat cream and sugar to a boil. Remove from heat, add chocolate, and whisk until smooth. Add egg yolks and whisk until incorporated. Pour into storage container, cover, and chill overnight.

Serves 6

Southpark's Banana Bread Pudding

Ingredients

- 2 *cups brown sugar, lightly packed*
- 1 *cup butter, room temperature*
- 4 *large eggs*
- 2 *cups mashed bananas, about 2 – 3 large bananas*
- 2 *teaspoons vanilla extract*
- ½ *cup sour cream*
- 2 *teaspoons ground cinnamon*
- ¼ *teaspoon grated nutmeg*
- ½ *teaspoon salt*
- 2 *teaspoons baking powder*
- 2 *teaspoons baking soda*
- 3½ *cups all purpose flour*
- *Bread Pudding Custard (recipe follows)*

Preparation

MAKE bread pudding custard.

TO MAKE the banana bread, begin by preheating the oven to 350 degrees. Butter a 9x13-inch glass baking dish. In a medium bowl, cream together brown sugar and butter for about 1 minute. Slowly add eggs and blend well. Add bananas, vanilla extract and sour cream and mix to combine. In a medium bowl combine all the dry ingredients then add to banana mixture, mixing just to combine. Pour into prepared baking dish and spread evenly. Bake in center of oven until a toothpick inserted in center comes out with moist crumbs attached, about 40 minutes. Best if made a day ahead. When cool, cut into ½ inch cubes and toast in 350 degree oven for 15-20 minutes until dry and toasted. Let cool.

BUTTER bottoms and sides of 8 8-ounce ramekins. In a large bowl combine the banana bread cubes and bread pudding custard, pushing down on the cubes to let the custard soak in. Let sit for half an hour, gently stirring occasionally to be sure all cubes are getting soaked. With a large slotted spoon, evenly divide the cubes into the prepared ramekins then pour the reserved custard into each ramekin to the top. Place ramekins in a large baking dish and add hot water into the dish until it reaches half way up sides of ramekins. Bake in a 325 degree oven, until custard is set, about 1½ hours. Let cool in water bath for half an hour, remove from water bath.

GENTLY unmold and place right side up on serving plate, or leave it in the ramekin. Serve with caramel sauce and vanilla bean ice cream, if desired.

For the Bread Pudding Custard

- 1¼ *cup granulated sugar*
- 10 *large eggs*
- 2½ *cups whole milk*
- 2½ *cups heavy whipping cream*
- ¼ *cup dark rum*
- 3½ *teaspoon vanilla extract*

IN A large bowl, whisk together sugar and eggs. Slowly whisk in cream and milk until thoroughly blended. Whisk in rum and vanilla extract. Store, covered, in refrigerator until ready to use.

Serves 8

Wine suggestion: pair with Blandy's Five Year Old Malmsey Madeira

Main entrance, Lewis and Clark Exposition - 1905.

Typhoon!

410 SW Broadway
(@ the Hotel Lucia)
503.224-8285
Portland, OR 97210
www.typhoonrestaurants.com

2310 NW Everett St.
503-243-7557

Monday – Friday
11:30 am - 2:00 pm
Monday – Thursday
5:00 pm - 9:00 pm
Friday – Saturday
5:00 pm - 10:00 pm
Sunday
4:30 pm - 9:00 pm

Typhoon!

Rated the "Best Pad Thai in Portland" by the Oregonian, this restaurant is a treat for lovers of pan-Asian cuisine. Steve and Bo Kline have created an ambience that is extremely inviting and laid the table with fantastic flavors.

Bo is short for Bongoj, which means Lotus in the Thai language. Bongoj Lohasawat was born in Bangkok, the daughter of a prominent highway engineer responsible for all the major roads in the provinces. She must have inherited her father's ambition. After graduating from Chulalongkorn, Thailand's most prestigious university, she earned a post-graduate degree at Eastern Washington University, and then studied for her doctorate at Gonzaga, specializing in Intercultural Communications. With this knowledge, she returned to Thailand, where her expertise was in high demand in the hotel industry. She created and supervised training programs for hotel employees and staff of all nationalities. In the early 1980's she started running the training programs for all new staff at the Bangkok Hilton, specialized in working with the diplomatic community and corporate sales at the new Shangri-La Hotel. In 1986, Bo took a position in charges of sales, marketing, and public relations for the first Amanpuri, which evolved into Asia's premier group of five-star resorts. In this position she traveled extensively to Hong Kong, Bangkok, Kuala Lumpur, Singapore, and Jakarta.

In 1988, Bo met her future husband, Steve Kline, who was in Bangkok making a movie. Steve's history was quite different than Bo's. Graduated from the University of Oregon with a BA in journalism, he led an early life that he describes as aimless, but served to set him up as a free-lance writer with national credits to his name, as well as working at The Oregonian and the LA Times.

While living in Los Angeles after marrying Steve, Bo began to emerge as a premier chef of Thai and pan-Asian cuisine, consulted by prominent restaurant owners and in demand by hostesses for parties and cooking classes. Looking for a place to raise their three children, Bo and Steve came back to the Northwest, where they have created another success with Typhoon!

Along with a fine selection of wine and beer, the Northwest District restaurant has an extensive list of fine teas. A second location, downtown at 400 SW Broadway, has a more sophisticated ambience, along with a full bar, as well as the same great marriage of flavors. Additional Typhoons are now located in Beaverton and Gresham Oregon and in Seattle and Redmond Washington.

Larb Chicken

Larb is a classic Thai salad that blends shrimp with lemon grass, toasted rice powder, and spices in a refreshing combination served with crisp lettuce leaves.

Ingredients

- 1 *cup minced chicken*
- ¼–½ *cup chicken broth*
- 1 *tablespoon sliced lemongrass (see notes-1)*
- 1 *tablespoon sliced shallots or red onion*
- 2 *tablespoons mint leaves*
- 1½ *teaspoon roasted rice powder (see notes-2)*
- 2 *tablespoons green onion*
- 2 *tablespoons chili flakes*
- 1 *tablespoon cilantro*
- *romaine lettuce (optional, for garnish)*
- *cabbage wedge (optional, for garnish)*
- *green beans (optional, for garnish)*
- *Larb Dressing (recipe follows)*

Preparation

HEAT chicken broth in a small saucepan over medium high heat. Stir in minced chicken to cook, keep breaking any big lumps that form. While chicken is cooking, make the dressing.

ONCE thoroughly cooked, drain chicken very well. Transfer cooked minced chicken to a small mixing bowl.

ADD the rest of the ingredients and toss with a quarter cup of larb dressing. To serve, garnish with romaine lettuce, a wedge of cabbage and green beans.

For the Larb Dressing

- 10 *tablespoons lime juice*
- 6 *tablespoons fish sauce*
- 1 *tablespoon sugar*
- ½ *teaspoon chili flakes*
- 1 *teaspoon roasted chili paste (see notes-3)*

MIX all ingredients together using wire whisk, making sure that sugar dissolves.

NOTES

1. When working with lemongrass, peel off the outer discolored hard leaves. Fresh lemongrass has pastel green color. Start slicing lemongrass ½ inch above the bottom part. Discard the top, which is the leafy part of lemongrass.
2. Roast rice grains in a wok over medium high heat. Keep stirring till rice turns golden brown. Grind in a coffee grinder or in a mortar.
3. Roasted chili paste in oil is easy to find in any Asian grocery store. If you cannot find this chili add ½ teaspoon chili flakes to the dressing, and you may need to add a little more sugar.

Serves 2-3 as appetizer

Wine suggestion: I'd recommend a crisp Alsatian Riesling. The spiciness of the dish balances the subtle sweetness to a point of perfection. Pinot Gris from Oregon, such as Cooper Mountain or Erath, also works well with this dish.

Eggplant Lover

My mother is the inspiration for this dish, having recalled it from the time she was a young girl. Chinese eggplant stir-fried with a delicate Thai black bean sauce served with tofu or shrimp. Popular perhaps 50 years ago, this historic dish was long forgotten until I researched it and interviewed a number of older cooks to recreate the recipe. It's one of the steady favorites on our menu.

Ingredients

- *8 ounces Chinese eggplant (don't use Japanese eggplant, which is more bitter)*
- *4-6 prawns, or firm tofu cut into bite size*
- *canola oil, enough for deep frying and stir frying*
- *1 teaspoon finely minced garlic*
- *1 teaspoon crushed and minced Thai chili*
- *1 teaspoon Thai fermented black beans (Tao Jiew)*
- *2 tablespoons oyster sauce*
- *dash of Thai light soy sauce*
- *1 teaspoon sugar*
- *¼ cup chicken broth or water*
- *¼ cup large julienne red bell pepper*
- *basil leaves (Thai, if possible)*

Preparation

TO PREPARE eggplants for stir fry, cut eggplants into 2-inch sections, then quarter lengthwise. Heat oil for deep frying in a wok until hot. Add eggplant (and cut tofu, if used) into oil to deep fry. Once eggplant pieces become a light golden brown and the color turns bright purple, remove from oil with slotted spoon and drain on a paper towel. Set aside.

TO STIR FRY, heat 1 tablespoon canola oil in a wok using medium high heat, add garlic, chili and fermented black beans. Stir quickly – do not let them burn. Once the ingredients start to give out aroma, toss in shrimp.

ONCE shrimp turns pink, add oyster sauce, Thai light soy sauce and sugar. Stir quickly. Add chicken broth or water as needed. We need enough sauce to toss with the prepared eggplant.

ADD julienned red bell pepper and basil. Stir quickly.

TOSS eggplant in with the sauce, turn off the heat. There should be some sauce left at the bottom of the pan – if not, add a little more chicken stock.

TO SERVE, arrange on platter and garnish with a sprig of basil.

Serves 2

Wine suggestions: We often recommend Penfold's Koonunga Hill Shiraz Cabernet. Also works well with a great Oregon Pinot Noir, such as Erath, Rex Hill, Archery Summit or one of the many great Australian Shiraz offerings.

Massaman Beef Curry

This is the most popular curry among Thais. It is also the heartiest and most time consuming kind of curry. The curry itself has stew-like textures with the aroma and flavors of dry-roasted spices e.g. cumin, caraway, cardamom, cinnamon, cloves, coriander seeds and nutmeg. Massaman has every element of Thai flavors; spicy, sweet, tangy but not sour, and salty. Through research, the name of the curry tells its origin: Muslim curry. In the south of Thailand there is a big population of muslims. In the 16th century the Portuguese introduced chili to southeast Asia and along came a lot of other spices and dishes. Some claimed that this curry came from Persia. Nevertheless, Thais have elevated the taste of the dish to another level.This dish always makes its way to the Typhoon special menu around Valentine's Day.

Ingredients

2 pounds stew beef
1 can coconut milk less 1 cup of the thick part
2 cups water
1 carrot, cut in chunks, approx 1 cup
1 medium sized potato, cut in chunks the same size as stew beef, approx 1 cup
1 cup onion
1 tablespoon peanuts
1 bay leaf (optional)
1 tablespoon fried shallots for additional flavor and garnish (optional)
1 tablespoon cardamom, wok roasted (optional)
Curry Sauce (recipe follows)

Preparation

IN A medium sized pot, cook beef in 1 can (less 1 cup) coconut milk and water for about 1 hour or until the meat is tender. Prepare curry sauce.

POUR the curry sauce into the beef pot and add carrots, potato, onion, peanuts and bay leaf.

THE CURRY is ready when the potatoes are totally cooked and meat is tender. The process takes 2 to 2½ hours.

ADD in fried shallot and roasted cardamom, then turn off the heat. Goes well served with jasmine rice.

For the Curry Sauce

3-4 tablespoons Massaman curry paste
2 tablespoons canola oil
1 cup thick coconut milk
6-7 tablespoons fish sauce
5 tablespoons tamarind juice
½ pound palm sugar

Massaman Beef Curry

CONTINUED

IN A small pan, over medium heat, add canola oil and curry paste. Stir to mix the curry paste with oil almost constantly till curry paste brightens in color and there are no lumps. Add thick coconut milk in the pan. Keep stirring with wire whisk to dissolve curry paste. Turn down the heat or add more liquid from the pot that the beef is cooking in, if necessary. Once the paste is dissolved, add the fish sauce, tamarind juice and palm sugar.

Serve 4–6

Wine suggestion: We often recommend Penfold's Koonunga Hill Shiraz Cabernet.
Also works well with a great Oregon Pinot Noir, such as Erath, Rex Hill, Archery Summit or one of the many great Australian Shiraz offerings.

VQ

1220 SW 1st Ave.
Portland, OR 97204
503-227-7342
www.veritablequandary.com

Monday – Friday
Lunch
11:30 am – 3:00 pm
Monday - Sunday
Dinner
5:00 pm – 10:00 pm
Saturday – Sunday
Brunch
9:30 am – 3:30 pm

Veritable Quandary

The history of this Portland landmark is fascinating. Originally a stonecutter's workshop, the building has served as an Oriental bathhouse, a residence for Portland's shipbuilders during World War II and, since 1970, the home of the Veritable Quandary. The restaurant's original and only owner, Dennis King started the business shortly after graduating from Portland State University. Being a penniless graduate, Dennis was lucky enough to find a mentor in the building's owner, Nels Peterson. Nels rented Dennis the building and then offered to help bankroll him if he had a sound business plan.

On January 19, 1971, the Veritable Quandary opened with the idea of creating a haven for young adults in downtown Portland, with service for beer and wine. In 1975, he added a dining room and a full liquor license. Once a right of passage for Portland's young drinking crowd, the VQ has gone through a metamorphosis. With the years, and the addition of several dining rooms, the restaurant offers 4 distinct dining areas, beside the beautiful patio artistically designed with lovely flowering plants. The original front section had a 22-foot antique wooden bar top that traveled around the Horn on a sailing ship. Unfortunately a tragic fire several years ago destroyed the bar and broke Dennis's heart. Not being one to give up, he and his staff started demolition and had a chance to redesign the structure to its present state. In the front section, the antique brick walls display historical pictures of Portland's riverside and frame the quaint wooden booths lining the bar. The second section is a delightful contrast with a huge atrium overlooking the patio. The third section is a few steps up, and probably would be considered a compromise between the two extremes, a cozy smaller room with a few tables and subdued lighting. The fourth interior section is a newly added private dining room in the 900-bottle wine cellar that can seat up to 8 guests.

Veritable Quandary's Chef, Anne Cuggino, took a while to get to Portland. Growing up in New York, she graduated from the prestigious Culinary Institute of America in Hyde Park, NY. After the 24-month program, she gained immeasurable experience at some of the top restaurants in the United States: the Union Square Café in NYC, and Mr. B's and Emeril's, both in New Orleans. Her first Sous Chef position was back in New York with Chef Chalres Kiley at The Abbey. All these experiences gave her an appreciation for using fresh, sustainable local ingredients. After moving to Portland in 1994, she was hired by Dennis King to revise the menu of the VQ. She enthusiastically took on the challenge and is responsible for the sumptuous menu available today.

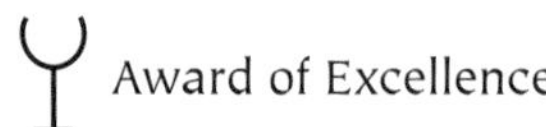

Award of Excellence

Stuffed Dates

appetizer

Ingredients

- 6 *pitted dates*
- 6 *Marcona almonds, fried*
- 6 *teaspoons peppered chèvre (use fresh black pepper)*
- 3 *strips of smoked bacon (half cooked so it is still pliable. Cut each slice in half)*
- *reduced Marsala (optional)*

Preparation

STUFF each date with an almond and a teaspoon of chèvre. Wrap each of them with a half slice of bacon and thread them onto a skewer. Grill them until they are crispy.

Best serve with a drizzle of reduced Marsala. To reduce Marsala, simmer it gently until it is syrupy.

Serves 2 as an appetizer

Pizza Crust

Ingredients

- 4 *cups bread flour*
- ¾ *cup course cornmeal*
- 1 *tablespoon kosher salt*
- 1½ *cups tepid water*
- 1 *tablespoon dry yeast, dissolved in ¼ cup warm water*
- 1 *tablespoon chopped fresh rosemary*
- 1 *tablespoon extra virgin olive oil*

Preparation

BRIEFLY mix together flour, cornmeal, and salt. Add water, yeast mixture and rosemary and olive oil. Knead for 10 minutes, and let it rise until double.

PUNCH down and shape into six tight 6-ounce balls. Flatten balls into disks and drizzle with olive oil. Let rest for 20 minutes. Stretch into rustic shapes as thin as possible without tearing. Grill on a hot grill. Drizzle the dough with more extra virgin olive oil as needed.

A COUPLE of our favorite toppings:

Gorgonzola and Pear:
BRUSH crust with extra virgin olive oil, dot with Gorgonzola and fresh sliced pear. Top with candied or toasted walnuts and fresh cracked black pepper. Bake until crispy.

OR

Smoked Salmon with Chèvre:
BRUSH crust with extra virgin olive oil, dot with fresh soft chèvre, flaked smoked salmon, thinly sliced red onion, and fried capers. Bake until crispy.

Makes 6 10" crusts

Osso Buco

Ingredients

- 6 *pounds veal shank*
- *salt and pepper to taste*
- *flour to dredge*
- *oil to sauté*
- 1 *onion*
- 1 *carrot*
- 1½ *ribs celery*
- ¼ *cup minced garlic*
- 10 *sprigs freshly chopped rosemary*
- 3¼ *cups canned San Marzano tomatoes*
- *approximately 1 quart of Italian red wine*
- *enough homemade veal stock to just cover the meat*

Preparation

GENEROUSLY salt and pepper both sides of veal shanks. Dredge in flour and sauté in olive oil to dark brown. Put browned shanks into heavy casserole dish and top with diced onion, carrot, celery, garlic and rosemary. Top with tomatoes last.

ADD wine to within an inch from top of meat, then add veal stock so the liquid just covers the meat. Cook in 400 degree oven until very tender, approximately three and a half hours. Skim fat from the top of the sauce. Goes well served over risotto, with grated Pecorino-Romano cheese and fresh basil.

Serves 6

Columbia Saloon.

andina
andina
andina
bar
lunch
dinner
1314 NW Glisan
Portland, OR 97209
503-228-9535
www.andinarestaurant.com
Sunday & Monday
Closed
Lunch
Tuesday-Saturday
11:30 am – 2:30 pm
Dinner
Tuesday-Thursday
5:30 pm - 9:30 pm
Friday-Saturday
5:30 pm – 10:30 pm
Tapas Tues-Sat.
11:30 am - close

andina

Andina restaurant is the product of a long and fruitful marriage between John and Doris Platt Rodriguez, representing two cultures fused into one project. During his time as a Peace Corps volunteer, John met Doris in her hometown of Cajamarca. He stayed a total of eleven years, sharing his native Oregon experience with Peru, and now the couple has come full circle, bringing the Peru influence to Oregon.

Andina opened in July of 2003 in Portland's chic Pearl district and the unique cuisine received favorable reviews. The restaurant is housed in an old Portland warehouse and features a large open atrium with a Spanish balcony dividing the formal dining area and tapas bar. The interior palette is warm, simple earth tones, which complement the exposed old Douglas fir ceiling beams and oak flooring. The wine rack is based on a design from the pre-Incan Chimu' culture of Peru's north coast. Colorful wall hangings and photos echo the visual appeal of the tasty dishes, served by a friendly, bi-lingual staff.

Andina serves authentic Peruvian fare, created by Executive Chef Emmanuel Piqueras Villaran, a native Peruvian and graduate of Le Cordon Bleu in Lima. After apprenticing at prestigious restaurants in Lima and Spain, Emmanuel received his formal certification as a chef. Emmanuel combines elements of all who have contributed to Peru's culinary milieu, including the indigenous, Spanish, French, Italian, Chinese, Japanese, and African. Some of the notable dishes include: cebiche (raw seafood cooked in a marinade of lime juice, onions, peppers and spices), chupes (Peruvian seafood soups) and causas (cold pastries of the coast), secos (hearty stews) and papas (hundreds of varieties of potato species) of the Andes, and fresh wild game. To complement dinner, select from a wide selection of fine wines from Chile and Argentina, beers and cocktails from Peru, or ports and sherry from Spain. Andina tops off its innovative food and drink with live Latin music on Friday and Saturday evenings.

Andina's goal is to establish a flagship enterprise for Peruvian and Novoandina cuisine for the Northwest and beyond. You won't want to miss a chance to sample the flavors, culture, and hospitality of this memorable dining experience.

andina atrium

Cebiche De Camarones

Shrimp Cebiche

Cebiche, Peru's flagship dish, is made of raw foods cooked in key lime juice (or other citrus juice) with a marinade of fresh onions, cilantro, hot pepper and sea salt. At andina we serve them in the traditional style with Cusco corn kernels, slices of camote (yam), and pieces of cancha (crispy corn nuggets).

Ingredients

8 fresh water shrimp
sea salt
1 tablespoon rocoto pepper, finely chopped
1 tablespoon cilantro, finely chopped
1 tablespoon garlic, pureed
1 tablespoon ginger, finely chopped
juice from 4 key limes
3 ounces aji amarillo puree
1 ounce red peppers, finely chopped
2 ounces red onion, julienned and kept in iced water
1 tablespoon chives
miner lettuce
mizuna mustard greens

Preparation

PLACE the shrimp in a pan and cover with water. Clean the shrimp, keeping the tail meat. Season the tails with salt, rocoto pepper, and cilantro. Then add the pureed garlic, the ginger, the aji Amarillo puree, and the lime juice. To assemble, place some miner lettuce and mizuna mustard greens at the bottom of a martini glass; add the shrimp mixture and decorate with red onion, red peppers and chives.

Serves 1 or serves 2 as an appetizer

Wine suggestion: A nice Pinot Gris, on the drier side, with its grassy, fruity aroma is a great match for a seafood cebiche like this one. A good alternative would be a young Sauvignon Blanc with a fruity bouquet.

Cazuela Cremosa De Quinoa Y Hongos

Quinoa and Mushroom Risotto

Quinoa is an ancient Inca grain rich in proteins and vitamins. It has a slightly nutty flavor and it can be used in preparations ranging from breakfast to the most elegant entree.

Ingredients

- *3 cups of mixed fresh/wild mushrooms*
- *2 teaspoons chopped garlic*
- *½ cup butter*
- *1 cup whipping cream*
- *6 cups cooked quinoa*
- *½ pound grated Parmesan cheese*
- *dash of white truffle oil*
- *24 green asparagus*
- *4 zucchini, sliced*
- *3 chilies, cubed*
- *salt to taste*
- *¼ cup olive oil*

Preparation

IN A saucepan, sauté the garlic in butter, then add mushrooms. Add the whipping cream and cook for four minutes until the cream absorbs the mushroom's flavor. Add the cooked quinoa and cook for five minutes. Add the Parmesan cheese and season to taste.

PLACE a ring mold on a serving dish, scoop the quinoa inside and slowly lift the ring. Sprinkle with a few drops of white truffle oil. Garnish with asparagus and zucchini slices, brushed with olive oil and grilled, and cubed chilies.

Serves 6

Wine suggestion: This entrée requires a good Merlot or a balanced Syrah to stand to the creaminess of the dish. Also a good Napa or Sonoma Zinfandel will work well.

Causa Rellena De Pollo

Chicken Causa

Causa is a typical dish from Lima that dates from the Colonial period. Its name is derived from the Quechua 'kausay' which translates as 'necessary substance'. Fresh lime-flavored potato mixture pressed into a cake, with savory fillings.

Ingredients

- *2 pounds yellow potato (Peruvian papa amarilla is best, but Yukon gold will work)*
- *3 aji amarillo (the paste is available at most Latin Food Markets)*
- *½ cup vegetable oil*
- *2 cloves of garlic*
- *2 key limes*
- *10 ounces cooked, boneless chicken breast*
- *½ cup mayonnaise*
- *1 small red onion*
- *2 hardboiled eggs*
- *6 olives*
- *6 butter lettuce leaves*
- *3 ounces fresh cheese (Cojito, or Farmers)*
- *chopped parsley*
- *salt and pepper to taste*

Preparation

BOIL the potatoes with salt to prevent cracking, then peel and mash into paste.
Saute the aji amarillo (or paste) in the oil, along with the garlic, then puree and add to potato paste, adding the juice from the key limes, salt and pepper and mixing and kneading until the mixture appears uniform.

PULL the chicken and add mayonnaise and chopped red onion for the filling.

TO ASSEMBLE, place a 3-4 inch cooking ring on a plate and fill ⅓ with potato paste, then a layer of filling, finishing with another layer of potato.

DECORATE with eggs, olives, lettuce, cheese, and parsley. Avocados, tomatoes, balsamic reduction, and other garnish can also be used, according to taste.

Serves 6

Wine suggestion: A wonderful match for this dish would be a South American or Australian Chardonnay, which tends to be less creamy or buttery than their French or American counterparts.

Escolar con Ravioli de Mango and Langostinos

Escolar Fish with Mango and Shrimp Ravioli

This is Chef Emmanuel Piqueras' masterpiece, and many people claim this is the best fish entrée they have ever had. It is a hearty fish entrée with fruit sauces.

Ingredients

- *6 ounces escolar fish*
- *4 shrimp*
- *⅜ cup aji panca paste*
- *2 tablespoons finely chopped ginger*
- *2 tablespoons ginger for broth*
- *1 tablespoon soy sauce*
- *1 tablespoon mirin*
- *1 mango*
- *½ tablespoon agar agar*
- *⅜ cup passion fruit juice*
- *⅜ cup cream cheese*
- *1 teaspoon turmeric*
- *2 cups onion broth*
- *3 tablespoons sugar*
- *2 tablespoons rocoto pepper*
- *½ tablespoon garlic*
- *½ cup fish stock*
- *½ tablespoon heavy cream*
- *1 carrot*
- *oil for cooking*
- *⅜ cup flour*
- *sea salt*
- *chives*

Preparation

CUT the fish into 4 cubes. Prepare a marinade with 1 tablespoon aji panca, half the minced ginger, soy sauce and mirin. Place the fish in the marinade and let rest for 2 hours. Slice the mango paper-thin using a mandolin or meat slicer. Then using a cutter, cut the slices into circles. Mix the agar agar and 2 tablespoons of warm passion fruit juice. Mix in the cream cheese with the turmeric. Blanch the shrimp in onion broth and 2 tablespoons ginger for one minute.

TO PREPARE the passion fruit honey sauce, place the remaining passion fruit juice in a saucepan. Add 2 tablespoons sugar, the rocoto pepper and the remaining minced ginger and cook on low heat for 20 minutes until it has the consistency of honey. In a separate saucepan, sauce the garlic and remaining aji panca, and add to the honey sauce. Reserve.

TO PREPARE the salsa marina, reduce the fish stock by half, then add a dash of cream, strain and season to taste. Reserve.

SLICE the carrot using a mandolin or meat slicer, roll it up, and secure with a toothpick. Fry in hot oil for 3 minutes or until crispy.

TO ASSEMBLE the ravioli, place a mango slice on a serving dish. Put a dollop of the cream cheese mixture on top, lay a shrimp over the cream cheese, and cover with another mango slice. Sprinkle sugar on top and caramelize using a torch. Repeat four times, aligning the ravioli in a straight line.

COAT the fish cubes in flour and fry in hot oil for about four minutes. Place a piece of fish next to each ravioli. Cover the fish with the salsa marina, and draw a line of passion fruit honey over the fish and ravioli. Place the fried carrot pieces in between the ravioli and the fish. Place chives on top and serve.

Serves 1

Wine Suggestion: A smokey, buttery Chardonnay or even a South American Syrah or Carmenere.

Escolar con Ravioli de Mango and Langostinos

Arroz Con Leche De Lucuma

Lucuma Rice Pudding

In the pre-Hispanic worldview, the lucuma was connected with fertility. Archaeological evidence shows that the lucuma grew in soils rich in nutrients that allowed for a variety of plants to prosper. The lucuma pulp is moist and floury, with a light, sweet taste.

Ingredients

- ½ *cup jasmine rice*
- 2 *cups water*
- 1 *cinnamon stick*
- 2 *whole cloves*
- 1 *cup pureed lucuma*
- 2 *cans (14 ounces each) evaporated milk*
- ½ *cup sugar*
- *ground cinnamon (garnish)*
- *whipped cream (garnish)*

Preparation

WASH the rice and drain thoroughly. In a 2-quart pot, bring the rice, water, cinnamon, and cloves just to a boil. Reduce to a simmer and cook until the water has been absorbed. Add the lucuma and bring back to a boil. Add the evaporated milk and the sugar. Bring to a boil, then reduce to a simmer until mixture is thick. Cool completely and chill. Sprinkle ground cinnamon and whipped cream.

*If lucuma can't be found, replace with a puree of cooked sweet potato, and replace the white sugar with brown sugar.

Serves 4

andina dining

Bluehour

In 2000, after almost ten years operating the famed Zefiro Restaurant, restaurateur Bruce Carey was ready for a change. When the opportunity to cornerstone the new headquarters of Wieden + Kennedy advertising agency came up in a dramatic location in the burgeoning neighborhood called the Pearl District, the decision was made to let Zefiro define the nineties and for the new restaurant to define the next decade.

Bruce teamed up with Chef Kenny Giambalvo and together conceptualized Bluehour. The restaurant has been received with more excitement and praise than any other in memory, well, at least not since Zefiro.

In last year's restaurant issue, Gourmet magazine called Bluehour "the most exciting restaurant in Portland...." with "the most sophisticated food in town."

Bluehour engages the diverse neighborhood crowd from the Pearl, and attracts people from all over who enjoy the glamorous space and the amazing, elegant and delicious food offered for lunch and dinner.

Chef Kenny Giambalvo creates Continental-Mediterranean cuisine, derived from his Italian heritage and classical French training. The fresh menu is printed daily.

Grapefruit and Bay Shrimp Salad

A refreshing, colorful, and simple salad - best served in November when ruby red grapefruits are in the peak of their season. This salad is the perfect starter or complement to so many dishes. The Pacific Coast provides the freshest bay shrimp all year round making this salad versatile in any kitchen. Substitute grapefruit for any other citrus like orange, blood orange or clementines.

Ingredients

- 1 *large ruby grapefruit*
- 4 *ounces fresh cooked bay shrimp*
- 6 *ounces haricots verts or string beans*
- 1 *rib of celery*
- 1 *bunch green onions (whites only)*
- 10 *mint leaves (approximately), sliced finely*
- ⅓ *cup grapefruit dressing*
- *salt and fresh ground black pepper, to taste*
- *Dressing (recipe follows)*

Preparation

PEEL and section the grapefruit. Squeeze the juice from the remaining core and reserve for the dressing. Cut each grapefruit section in half.

TRIM the ends of the haricots verts or string beans. In a pot of boiling salted water cook the beans until tender but still slightly al dente. Shock in an ice water bath. Drain the beans when cooled and set aside.

PEEL the rib of celery. Slice the celery on the bias about an eighth of an inch thick. Blanch in boiling salted water for less then one minute. Shock in the ice water bath, drain, and set aside.

SLICE the green onion very thin.

IN A large mixing bowl toss all of the ingredients together with the dressing. Season to taste. Arrange the salad on plates and serve immediately.

For the Dressing

- ⅜ *cup fresh grapefruit juice*
- *zest of one grapefruit*
- 2 *tablespoons champagne vinegar*
- 1 *medium shallot, finely chopped*
- 1 *clove of garlic, finely chopped*
- 1 *teaspoon Dijon mustard*
- 1 *tablespoon chopped fresh tarragon*
- 1½ *cups olive oil*
- *salt and ground black pepper*

IN A food processor or blender, place all of the ingredients, except the olive oil. While turned on (if using a blender, run on medium speed) slowly add the olive oil. When all of the oil has been added, adjust the seasoning. This makes two cups of dressing, which can be made up to two days in advance and kept refrigerated.

Serves 4

Wine suggestion: Oregon Pinot Gris or Sparkling Wine

Mushroom Risotto Recipe

The abundance of delicious mushrooms produced in Oregon makes this dish a favorite for any season. Choose local varieties such as: morel, porcini, chanterelle, lobster, hedgehog or an assortment of crimini, shiitake or oyster. The combinations are endless and a mixture of any of these mushrooms works beautifully in this delicious, earthy, and classic risotto recipe.

Ingredients

4 ounces shiitake mushroom caps, sliced
4 ounces crimini mushroom caps, sliced
4 ounces oyster mushrooms, cleaned
4 ounces porcini mushrooms, sliced
1 medium yellow onion, minced very fine
olive oil for cooking
1 pound vialone nano rice
2 cups dry white wine
½ cup chopped Italian parsley
grated Reggiano Parmesan cheese
butter
salt and pepper
Vegetable Broth (recipe follows)

Preparation

IN A sauté pan, heat some olive oil until almost smoking. Add one type of mushroom and sauté quickly until tender. Remove the mushrooms and set aside. Continue this step until all of the mushrooms are cooked.

IN A heavy bottom saucepot, sweat the onions until very tender, but do not allow to brown. Add the rice and continue cooking, while stirring constantly, until the rice is sufficiently toasted.

ADD all of the wine and continue stirring until the wine is absorbed. Add all of the cooked mushrooms and blend with the rice. Adding just enough vegetable broth to cover the rice, continue cooking the rice until the broth is absorbed. Repeat this step until the rice is just tender or "al dente".

ADD enough broth to get a creamy consistency. Bring to a simmer and turn off the heat. Add the cheese and butter and stir into the rice vigorously. Adjust the seasoning and finish the risotto with the chopped parsley. Serve immediately.

For the Vegetable Broth

1 medium yellow onion, sliced
1 rib of celery, sliced
1 medium carrot, sliced
3 cloves of garlic
1 pound of mushroom stems and trimmings
olive oil for cooking
1 quart vegetable stock
bouquet of thyme, rosemary, sage and bay leaf
salt and pepper, to taste

SWEAT the onions, celery, carrot, garlic, and mushrooms in olive oil until onions are transparent. Add the vegetable stock, herbs, salt, and pepper and simmer for 20 - 30 minutes. Strain through a fine strainer and set aside.

Serves 6

Wine suggestion: Pinot Noir

Nido di Pasta

"Nido" meaning "nest" is a traditional dish served in the Piedmont region of Northern Italy. As a featured pasta dish at bluehour, it balances and showcases both local ingredients and its Italian roots. Nido works well as a pasta course or as an amusé. The richness and creaminess will leave an unforgettable impression on any palette.

Ingredients

½ pound all-purpose flour
8 egg yolks
½ pound porcini mushrooms
½ pound fresh ricotta
nutmeg to taste
salt and black pepper

1 cup pesto
2 cups vegetable stock
8 ounces sweet butter
1 cup grated Parmesan
salt and black pepper
1 teaspoon truffle oil, optional

Preparation

PREPARE the pasta dough by measuring flour into a mixing bowl. Make a well in the middle of the flour and measure the egg yolks into the well. Slowly incorporate the flour into the egg yolks until the dough is formed. Knead the dough by hand until smooth. Let rest.

USING a pasta machine, roll the dough out into sheets approximately 1⁄16 inch thick and 10 inches long and as wide as the machine allows.

BLANCH the sheets in boiling, salted water. Drain and toss in olive oil and set aside to cool. These sheets can be held up to 1 day in advance at this stage.

SLICE the porcinis and sauté in olive oil. Season with salt and pepper. Set aside.

STIR the ricotta in a mixing bowl by hand until creamy. Season the ricotta with salt and pepper and pinch of nutmeg.

PREPARE the pesto in classical style.

SPREAD the sheets out on a clean surface. Place a tablespoon of pesto in the center of each sheet and spread evenly, leaving ¼ inch border on all sides. Lay an even layer of the porcinis and finish with an even layer of the fresh ricotta.

FOLD in the right/left sides 3 inches. Starting at the side closest to you, roll the nido away from you, while keeping it tight (about 1-½ inch diameter).

WRAP each nido in plastic wrap. Tie off each end to make it airtight.

WHEN ready to serve, place the nido back in boiling salted water. Cook between 3-5 minutes. Cut the plastic wrap. Remove the nido and cut into 5 equal parts and arrange.

AT THE same time, prepare the sauce by bringing the vegetable stock to a boil while whisking in the butter. Adjust the seasoning. Whisk in Parmesan. Turn fire off. Finish with truffle oil. Spoon the sauce over the pasta. Serve immediately.

Serves 4

Suggested Oregon Wine: Pinot Noir

23rd and Burnside ca. 1910.

Fratelli

fratelli

1230 NW Hoyt St.
Portland, OR 97209
503-241-8800
www.fratellicucina.com

Sunday – Thursday
5:30 pm – 9:00 pm
Friday – Saturday
5:30 pm – 10:00 pm

Halibut with Rhubarb and Asparagus

Fratelli

The words "Italian kitchen" sums up the approach at Fratelli. Instead of offering the predictable selections often associated with the words "Italian food," Fratelli re-creates the concept of the Italian kitchen, with fresh foods, creative combinations, and innovative surprises.

Executive chef and co-owner Paul Klitsie opened Fratelli in 1998 with his business partner, Tim Cuscaden. Located in the Pearl district of Portland, Fratelli's reputation quickly spread as people discovered the difference.

Comments about Fratelli include SavvyDiner.com: "...One of the Pearl District's most intriguing options. Complex regional Italian cuisine you won't find anywhere else...". The Oregonian wrote, "...Fratelli's interpretation of the culinary landscape is nearly flawless, with tempting discoveries in every course..."

Willamette Week said "...The ambience is very 'downtown'with a straightforward, unadorned touch that puts the emphasis just where it should be: on the food...". And OregonLive.com wrote "Authentic & adventurous, Fratelli brings simplicity & seriousness to the table."

Paul Klitsie received his training at the Hotelberufsfachschule Speiser in Germany and the cooking school in Groningen, Netherlands. He apprenticed at critically acclaimed restaurants in the Netherlands, Switzerland, and Germany and was the executive chef at Restaurant Vasso in Amsterdam.

Paul believes in combining only a few ingredients to bring out the natural flavors in each dish. Knowing that the best ingredients are found locally, Paul orchestrates Saluté! Summer, a weekly culinary feast featuring home-grown Oregon products such as fresh lamb, field greens, and exotic mushrooms. But any time of year, Fratelli is a delightful experience.

Crespelle alla Genovese

Crepes with Pesto and Arugula

Ingredients

4 large eggs
1 cup whole milk
1 cup all-purpose flour
5 tablespoons melted butter
1 bunch arugula
Pesto (recipe follows)

Preparation

MAKE pesto.

FOR the crepes, break the eggs into a metal bowl and whisk until loose. Stir in the milk. While continuing to whisk, sift in the flour and then add the melted butter. Stir or beat the batter until it is smooth. Strain it through a sifter to remove any lumps. Store the batter in a cool place for about an hour.

ONCE cooled, stir the batter with a 2-ounce ladle. The batter should have the consistency of a warm sauce - if the batter is too thick, add some milk.

PLACE a large sauté pan over high heat until it is medium hot - then adjust the heat to medium. Lightly butter the bottom of the pan. While holding the pan at an angle, spoon the crepe batter onto the highest point of the pan with the 2-ounce ladle. Turn the pan slightly to cover the bottom of the pan with batter. If necessary, add a little more batter. Put the pan back over medium heat and cook the crepe. When the batter has dried on one side, flip it over and cook for another 10 seconds. Slide the crepe onto a cold plate and repeat the process until you have six crepes.

TO SERVE, bring the crepes to room temperature and spread the pesto over the crepes using the back of a soup spoon. Then, sprinkle the arugula over the crepes and serve immediately.

For the Pesto

3 medium cloves of garlic, peeled
2 tablespoons roasted pine nuts
3 tablespoons grated Parmesan cheese
1 bunch of fresh basil, leaves only pinch of salt
1 cup extra virgin olive oil

BLEND the garlic and pine nuts in a food processor for a few seconds. Add the basil leaves and salt, and blend for another five seconds. While the machine is still on, slowly add the olive oil until the mixture has a sauce consistency. Then, add the Parmesan cheese - this will thicken the pesto.

REMOVE the mixture from the processor and place in a cool (not cold) place for at least an hour.

Serves 6

Grilled Green and Red Onion Ravioli Filling

Ingredients

- 3 *bunches of washed green onions, without the root part*
- 1½ *red onion, peeled*
- ½ *pound fresh mascarpone*
- 4 *tablespoons grated Parmigiano cheese*
- ½ *bunch marjoram, leaves only*
- *salt and pepper to taste*
- *olive oil*

Preparation

TAKE the end away from the green onions and season the rest with salt and pepper and a little bit of olive oil and grill them, making sure the onions get proper grill marks. Then set them aside. Halve the red onions from top to bottom and slice them in half rings about ⅛ of an inch thick, season them with salt and pepper and a little bit of olive oil, put them on the grill or grill pan, making sure they get proper grill marks. Put them aside.

PLACE the green and the red onions on a sheet pan and cook in the oven at 425 degrees for about 10 minutes or until they are soft and tender. Be careful that they don't burn!

COMBINE onions in a food processor along with the mascarpone, marjoram and grated cheese until you have a smooth mixture. Salt and pepper if necessary.

REMOVE the mixture from the food processor and spread it out on a plate, cover with plastic food wrap and let cool in the refrigerator.

USE the directions from a pasta book on how to make ravioli and use this filing for it.

SERVE cooked ravioli in melted butter with sliced marjoram leaves and grated Parmigiano.

Serves 6

Halibut with Rhubarb and Asparagus

Ingredients

- 1 *stick unsalted butter*
- 1½ *pounds rhubarb, red part washed and sliced into 1 inch sections*
- ½-¾ *cup granulated sugar*
- ½ *cup water*
- 2 *bunches thin stemmed asparagus*
- *extra virgin olive oil*
- 6 *6-ounce portions halibut*
- *salt and pepper for seasoning*

Preparation

MELT butter over medium heat in a heavy bottom saucepan, add the rhubarb before the butter changes color and stir it with a wooden spoon for 30 seconds, then add a half cup of sugar and the water. Stir in the sugar, temper the heat by half and put a lid on the pot. After about 10 minutes, the rhubarb will fall apart and should have a sauce-like thickness. If needed, add the rest of the sugar to taste. The flavor should be both tart and sweet. Take from heat and keep warm by leaving the lid on.

FOR the asparagus, remove the "wooden" part. Blanch the asparagus until there is still some bite left and shock them in ice water. Remove them and sprinkle with olive oil and season to taste. When ready to serve, you can reheat them in a hot oven (about 450 degrees) for 3-4 minutes, or grill the asparagus for 2-3 minutes.

FOR the halibut, season each portion with salt and pepper. Bring two large sauté pans to high heat and add the olive oil, sauté the fish crisp and gold colored on both sides, leave the inside of the fish at medium to medium rare temperature or as desired.

TO SERVE, divide the warm rhubarb over six plates, place the halibut on top and drape three to four asparagus over the fish. Drizzle lightly with extra virgin olive oil.

Serves 6

Pollo al Prosciutto con Polenta e Sugo di Funghi

Chicken wrapped in Prosciutto with Polenta and Mushroom Jus

Ingredients

- 6 *medium chicken breasts, preferably with skin*
- *salt and pepper, to taste*
- 6 *tablespoons olive oil*
- 6 *slices of prosciutto*
- *Polenta (recipe follows)*
- *Mushroom Jus (recipe follows)*

Preparation

PREHEAT the oven to 425 degrees.

MAKE the mushroom jus. Season the chicken breasts on both sides with salt and pepper. Bring two large sauté pans to high heat and add 3 tablespoons of olive oil to each. Place the chicken breasts skin-side down on the pan and sear until the skin is brown and begins to get crispy. Then, flip the breasts; color this side to a golden brown. If needed, add more oil.

IN THE meantime, lay each slice of prosciutto flat onto a flat surface. Lower the heat and remove the chicken from the pan and place each piece into the middle of a prosciutto slice. Fold the end pieces of the prosciutto over the chicken. Put the chicken on the skin side back in the pan, and then place both pans in the oven. Bake the chicken until done - the prosciutto and the skin will get crispy.

REMOVE the chicken from the pans. Make the polenta.

TO SERVE, divide the polenta mixture into six warm pasta bowls. Place the chicken on top of the polenta and pour 4 tablespoons of the warm mushroom jus over each plate.

For the Polenta

- 2 *ounces butter*
- 1 *shallot, diced*
- 1 *clove garlic, diced*
- 1½ *teaspoons rosemary, minced*
- ½ *teaspoon thyme, minced*
- ½ *teaspoon crushed chili peppers*
- 3 *cups chicken stock*
- 1 *cup whole milk*
- 1 *teaspoon salt*
- 1½ *cups polenta grits*
- ⅓ *cup Parmesan cheese, grated*

MELT 1 ounce of the butter in a heavy stockpot over medium heat. Add the shallot and garlic and sauté for 1-1½ minutes, or until they have a slight glaze. Add the rosemary, thyme and peppers and stir for about 30 seconds. Add the chicken stock, milk and salt and bring to a boil. Once it has reached a boil, whisk in the polenta until the mixture thickens. Reduce the heat to low and stir occasionally with a wooden spoon. It will take about 20 to 30 minutes for the polenta to cook - it will be thick and creamy, and the flavors will be subtly blended. Once cooked, use the wooden spoon to stir in the remaining 1 ounce butter and the grated Parmesan cheese until dissolved. Serve immediately.

Mushroom Jus

1 pint of button mushrooms
3-5 tablespoons olive oil, to taste
1 tablespoon extra virgin olive oil
3 large, peeled shallots, diced
3 cloves garlic, diced
3 cups chicken stock
salt and pepper, to taste

PUT the mushrooms in a food processor and pulse three or four times until they are chopped. Place a sauté pan over high heat and add 3 tablespoons olive oil to the pan. Add the mushrooms to the pan and stir occasionally with a wooden spoon to prevent the mushrooms from burning. After the mushrooms have some color, add the tablespoon of extra virgin olive oil and the shallots and garlic.

GIVE this mixture another minute to sauté and then deglaze it with the chicken stock and let it reduce by half. Turn the heat off and bring the contents of the pan over to a strainer and sift the mushrooms from the liquid. To maximize the liquid, press the mixture into the strainer with a ladle. Discard the mushroom pulp. Season the jus with salt and pepper, to taste.

Serves 6

Fennel and Cumin Seed Cured Pork Tenderloin
recipe on following page.

Fennel and Cumin Seed Cured Pork Tenderloin

Ingredients

6 7-ounce pork tenderloins
1 tablespoon fennel seed, ground
1 tablespoon cumin seed, ground
1 teaspoon black pepper, ground
2 tablespoons curing salt
¾ cup olive oil
6 tablespoons butter
2 bunches baby carrots, peeled and green removed
½ pound fresh, peeled fava beans
2 medium sized green zucchinis
2 peeled parsnips
water and salt
2 balls of fresh mozzarella, cut into five slices each
Jus (recipe follows)

Preparation

MIX the fennel and cumin seed with the pepper and the curing salt. Slice the end part of the loins so that you will have 6 similar loins, put the curing mixture over the loins, rub the curing mixture into the meat. Wrap the loins individually in plastic and put them in the refrigerator for about 12 hours.

PREPARE the vegetables. Bring a generous amount of water to a boil in a stock pot and add about a teaspoon of salt to the water. When the water is at a rolling boil, add the carrots and blanch them for about two minutes. Take them out of the water and put them in ice water so they get a beautiful orange color.

DOUBLE peel the fava beans. Take the bean out of the big shell. Bring a stock pot filled with water to a rolling boil. Add a teaspoon of salt and then add the beans. Blanch them for 2 minutes and then put them in ice water. When the beans are cold, carefully take the next skin off with a knife. When this is removed you will have a beautiful hard green colored bean with a slightly sweet and bitter flavor.

RINSE the zucchinis and dry them with a towel, then cut the top and the bottom part off about 1½inches on each side. Slice the zucchini lengthwise into two parts and repeat this again with the two halves. When this is done, put the zucchini with the green side down and you will see a separation between the seeds and the flesh of the vegetable. Follow this line with your knife and remove the seeds, having left over the flesh of the zucchini, repeat this procedure with every piece. Then sprinkle the eight pieces with olive oil, season them with salt and pepper and grill them for about 3 minutes total, about 1½ minutes on each side and let them cool off. Then slice the pieces into 1 inch thick parts.

CUT the parsnip the same way lengthwise as the zucchini. When this is done, put your knife diagonally on the parsnip half and slice about ¼ inch thick. Using a sauté pan over high heat, add olive oil to the pan and add half of the sliced parsnip. Sauté the parsnips for about four minutes and stir with a wooden spoon in the pan to prevent burning. Season the parsnip and turn off the heat, then add 4 tablespoons of white wine. Let this evaporate and take the parsnips out of the pan. Clean the pan and repeat the same procedure with the other half of the parsnips.

REMOVE the loins and shake off excessive curing mixture. Put a large sauté pan over high heat and add half of the oil. When hot, add the loins and sear them on each side for about a minute, then lower the heat to medium and add the butter. Total cooking time is about 8 minutes or to your own preferable temperature. Take the loins out of the pan and let them rest for about three minutes.

HEAT a medium sized heavy bottom stockpot over medium heat and add 4 tablespoons of extra virgin olive oil to the pan. Then add parsnip, carrots, zucchini and the fava beans. Stir the vegetables with a wooden spoon. When they are hot, add the mozzarella and immediately divide the vegetables among the six plates. If you wait too long, the mozzarella melts and will form long threads of cheese. Put the slices of pork on top of the vegetables and ladle the jus over the meat. Serve immediately.

For the Jus

1 tablespoon tomato paste
¼ cup red wine
2 cups beef broth
2 tablespoons unsalted butter
salt and pepper to taste
1 teaspoon fresh chopped savory herb

BRING the pan in which you sautéed the meat to medium heat and add the tomato paste. Stir immediately with a wooden spoon to prevent burning. After half a minute, add the red wine, mix it with the tomato paste and add the beef broth. Reduce by half, then lower the heat. Add the butter, keep on stirring until the butter is completely dissolved. Add the herb, check the taste and, if necessary, season with salt and pepper.

Serves 6

Entrance to Chinatown.

In Good Taste

231 NW 11th Ave.
Portland, OR 97209
503-248-2015
www.ingoodtastestore.com

Retail store hours
Monday-Friday
10 am – 6 pm
Saturday
10 am – 6 pm
Sunday
Noon – 5 pm

In Good Taste

In Good Taste Cooking School is one of Portland's best cooking schools, located in the fashionable Pearl district. In Good Taste provides everything a person needs to entertain in style, from cooking classes to full catering services.

The director of the In Good Taste School, Ron Glanville, began his culinary training in the early '70's, when he studied under Joyce Goldstein in San Francisco, California and James Beard in Venice, Italy and New York City. He worked in restaurants and catering companies in New York, Connecticut, and California. He enrolled in the Horst Mager Culinary Institute in Portland, then became the Executive Chef at the Couch Street Fish House during the 1980s.

He went to the Western Culinary School, where he taught International Cuisine. In the '90s, Ron became a private chef, emphasizing classic style with Northwest and Mediterranean influences. His philosophy is that fresh and ripe products should never be overwhelmed or lose their delicate flavor. Food should reflect truth and beauty.

The cooking classes are an educational experience, with each course carefully paired with wine. There is either a Hands On or a demonstration of a menu, and the instructor focuses on techniques, tools, and ingredients used in preparing the dishes. Classes include a full multi-course meal with wine tasting. Friday night wine dinners combine regional meals paired with appropriate wine flights.

There are also classes for kids, which teach the basics, including browning, boiling, grilling, sautéing, and baking, along with kitchen safety and sanitation.

In Good Taste is a place for people who are passionate about food and wine.

Les Gougères

Ingredients

1 *cup water*
3 *ounces unsalted butter*
1 *teaspoon salt*
1 *cup all purpose flour*
1 *cup eggs, mixed thoroughly in a bowl*
½ *cup gruyere cheese, grated*
½ *cup Parmesan cheese, grated*
egg wash (1 egg to 1 tablespoon water, blended)

Preparation

IN A 2 quart pan bring water to boil, add butter, salt, and flour. Stir with a wooden spoon until the mixture comes together into a ball, and roast the ball until a film forms off of the bottom of the pan. Pour ball into the mixing bowl and beat at medium speed. Slowly add eggs and beat until the mixture comes together. Add cheese and blend. Turn into pastry bag and pipe small evenly sized balls onto the sheet.

BRUSH with the egg wash, and bake in a preheated 425 degree oven for 20 minutes until doubled in size and golden.

Makes about 30 gougères

Braised Broccoli Rabe in Cream Sauce

Ingredients

2 *tablespoons olive oil*
1 *yellow onion, diced*
2 *cloves of garlic, finely chopped*
2 *bunches broccoli rabe*
½ *cup white wine*
½ *cup of cream*
salt and pepper to taste

Preparation

HEAT a sauté pan over medium heat, add the olive oil and sauté the onion until softened but not brown, add the garlic and the broccoli rabe, and sauté for 5 minutes. Add the wine and deglaze the pan. Lower the heat and cover tightly. Cook for 15 minutes, add the cream, and reduce to sauce consistency. Season to taste and serve.

Serves 8

Gazpacho

Cold Spanish Tomato and Vegetable Soup

Ingredients

- *1 cup red onions, chopped*
- *1 cup green bell pepper, cored, seeded and chopped*
- *1 cup cucumber, peeled, seeded and chopped*
- *1 cup tomatoes, peeled and chopped*
- *1½ teaspoons garlic, chopped*
- *1½ teaspoons kosher salt*
- *¼ teaspoon sweet pimenton (Spanish Paprika)*
- *¼ teaspoon cayenne*
- *¼ cup tomato paste*
- *1 tablespoon white wine vinegar*
- *¼ cup extra virgin olive oil*
- *1 tablespoon fresh lemon juice*
- *3 cups tomato juice or V8*
- *sprigs of thyme, for garnish*
- *chopped parsley, for garnish*
- *croutons of baguette, brushed with oil and baked, fried or grilled, for garnish*

Preparation

BLEND all the ingredients in a blender or food processor until the gazpacho is smooth. Refrigerate the gazpacho until ready to serve. Garnish with chopped parsley, sprigs of thyme, and croutons.

Serves 8

Goat Cheese Flan

Ingredients

5 eggs, lightly beaten
½ cup soft goat cheese
2 cups milk, scalded
1 teaspoon shallots, chopped
salt and pepper to taste

Preparation

PREHEAT oven to 350 degrees. Butter individual 4-ounce soufflé dishes, and prepare a bain marie: a shallow baking pan that will easily fit all of the soufflé dishes.

IN A bowl, combine the eggs and the goat cheese, mixing well. Temper (gradually adding hot milk, while whisking) milk into egg mixture; add chopped shallots and season with salt and pepper.

LADLE mixture into prepared baking dishes and place into bain marie. Slowly and carefully add hot water around the dishes until half way up the sides of the pan and dishes. Place in the 350 degree oven and bake for 30 minutes.

GOES well with a mixed green salad with light flavored vinaigrette.

Serves 8

Mussels in Saffron Cream Sauce

Ingredients

- 1 *cup white wine*
- 2 *pounds live mussels, cleaned*
- *generous pinch of saffron threads*
- 2 *tablespoons unsalted butter*
- 3 *tablespoons shallots, minced*
- 1 *cup heavy cream*
- 1 *tablespoon unsalted butter, chilled and cut into small cubes*
- *salt and ground white pepper, to taste*
- 2 *tablespoons chopped parsley*

Preparation

IN A large pot, bring the wine to boil, place the mussels into the liquid and cover with a tight lid. Cook for 4 to 5 minutes until the mussels are open. Drain and reserve the liquid. Discard any mussels that have not opened.

INFUSE the wine-mussel liquor with the saffron threads.

IN A heavy skillet, heat the butter and sweat the shallots. Add the reserved saffron liquid from the steaming of the mussels then add the heavy cream. Simmer for 10 minutes until the liquid is reduced and it is a thick mixture. Whisk butter into sauce to emulsify. Season for taste.

REMOVE half of the mussel shell and free the meat so that it sits easily in the remaining shell, arrange onto heated plates. Spoon some sauce onto each mussel. Sprinkle with parsley.

Serves 6

Cabernet Sauvignon Braised Lamb

with Root Vegetables

Ingredients

- 10 *ounces bacon, cut into lardoons*
- 4 *tablespoons olive oil*
- 2 *pounds onion, chopped*
- 3 *carrots, peeled and cut into large dice*
- 3 *stalks of celery, peeled and cut into large dice*
- 3 *parsnips, cut into large dice*
- 4 *pounds lamb, cut into cubes*
- *salt to taste*
- 4 *tablespoons flour*
- 4 *cups of Cabernet Sauvignon or other red wine*
- 2 *tablespoons tomato paste*
- 2 *teaspoons fresh thyme leaves*
- *bouquet garnie (2 rosemary sprigs and 4 sage leaves, wrapped in cheese cloth)*
- *ground black pepper, to taste*
- *Egg Noodles (recipe follows)*

Preparation

IN A large casserole, put 4 tablespoons of olive oil, add the bacon, and render until slightly brown. Remove the bacon with a slotted spoon and reserve. Add the onions to the casserole and cook until they begin to color. Add the carrots, celery, and parsnips and cook until they start to get a little color. Remove vegetables with a slotted spoon and reserve with the bacon. Add the lamb to the casserole and brown on all sides, salting them as you go. Sprinkle the flour over the lamb, and continue to cook until the flour begins to brown. Return the vegetables and bacon to the pan and deglaze with the wine, add the tomato paste, and herbs. Bring to a boil then reduce the heat to a simmer, cover and cook until the lamb is tender, about 2½ hours, or put pan in a 325 degree oven for 2 – 3 hours.

WITH a slotted spoon remove all the meat and vegetables to a dish, reduce the liquid to sauce consistency, and adjust seasoning with salt and pepper. Pour the sauce over the lamb and serve with egg noodles.

For the Egg Noodles

- 2 *pounds egg noodles*
- 1½ *gallons salted water*
- 3 *tablespoons unsalted butter*

IN A large pot bring the water to a boil, add the egg noodles, and cook until al dente. Drain and toss with butter. Serve immediately.

Serves 8 - 10

Mt. Tabor Train on 6th St., Portland - late 1880's.

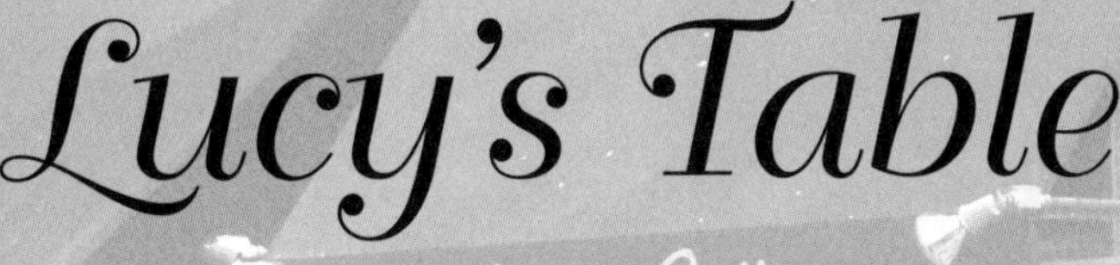

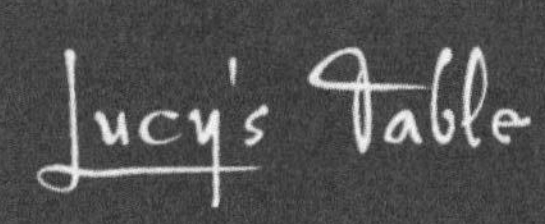

704 NW Irving St.
Portland, OR 97209
503-226-6126
www.lucystable.com

Dinner
Monday - Saturday
5:00 pm 'til closing

Lucy's Table

Peter & Kelly Kost opened Lucy's table in 1998. Lucy's is a friendly restaurant with a relaxed ambiance. Located on North Irving in the upscale Northwest District of Portland, the dining room is a comfortable setting, with white linen tablecloths and comfortable ladder-back chairs. The large windows framed with black velvet offer pleasant views of the tree-lined street, and are shaded by large black awnings. These awnings also spread over the tables that are arranged for outside seating in the summer. A small bar adjoins the dining room and, in the evening, the amber-hued lighting invites an atmosphere of coziness and intimacy without being subdued.

Peter and Kelly named their restaurant after Peter's maternal grandmother, the quintessential Italian "Nonna" who showed her love through cooking. "She was a great cook - no one wanted to miss a meal at Nonna's," Kost says. He and Kelly strive to make guests feel that way about Lucy's Table. "Having guests return time and again - we couldn't ask for better recognition of our work."

Chef Dylyn Coolidge and his staff use only the freshest produce, seafood, meats and game to create his dishes. The menu specializes in dishes that have French country and northern Italian influences. The menu varies each month to take advantage of the bounty of each season. Lucy's is known for their signature dishes. Goat Cheese Ravioli with Crispy Shallots & Pancetta or Roasted Red Beet & Pear Salad would be a great way to start your dining experience. The Wild Boar Tagliatelle is a constant favorite, with its meat braised until tender in a rich stock of red wine, herbs and vegetables, served over fresh tagliatelle pasta, and topped with Pecorino Romano and orange gremolata. Or, try the Duck Risotto with wild mushrooms, Parmesan, foie gras butter and Carnaroli rice.

To complement the succulent taste of the cuisine, owner Peter Kost maintains an extensive wine list from Europe, South America, Australia and the United States.

Cucumber, Melon, and Grape Gazpacho

Ingredients

2 English cucumbers, peeled
1 honeydew melon, seeded and peeled
1 bunch white seedless grapes
1 clove garlic, chopped fine
½ cup crustless white bread, cubed
½ cup celery, peeled and chopped
2 tablespoons Vidalia onion, chopped
1 tablespoon mint, chopped
1 tablespoon Italian parsley, chopped
½ cup Champagne vinegar
½ cup extra virgin olive oil
salt and pepper to taste
Italian Moscato d'Asti

Preparation

PLACE bread in water for 5 minutes, then squeeze out water by hand. Put bread in blender with cucumbers, melon, grapes, garlic, white bread, celery, onion, mint, parsley, and Champagne vinegar. Puree until smooth. When smooth, slowly add the olive oil. Season with salt and pepper to taste.

DRIZZLE about a quarter cup cold Moscato d'Asti over each individual bowl just before serving. Gazpacho should be served chilled.

Serves 8

Goat Cheese Ravioli

Ingredients

- 1 *pound goat cheese chevre*
- 1 *egg*
- 1 *tablespoon bread crumbs*
- *salt to taste*
- *white pepper to taste*
- 1 *package of 3x3 inch wonton skins*
- 1 *egg, beaten*
- ½ *pound pancetta*
- ½ *pound Parmesan Reggiano*
- *Italian parsley and chives, equal parts, chopped*
- *Brown Butter Sauce (recipe follows)*

Preparation

MIX goat cheese, egg, bread crumbs, salt, and pepper with a mixer that has a paddle attachment (this can be done by hand with large spoon), until well incorporated. Spoon one tablespoon of stuffing onto the center of each wonton square. Brush edges of wonton squares with beaten egg to hold sides together. Fold over edges of wonton to make a triangle. Seal by pressing gently with tines of fork. Drop ravioli into boiling water. When they float they are done.

DICE the pancetta ¼ inch, render in olive oil over low heat till crispy. Serve with grated Parmesan, fried pancetta, chopped herbs, and brown butter sauce.

Brown Butter Sauce

- ½ *pound salted butter*
- ½ *pound unsalted butter*
- 1½ *quarts heavy cream*

HEAT butter on medium heat until light brown. Add cream and whisk, heating until it thickens.

Serves 10

Cocoa-Espresso Rubbed Lamb

with Polenta, Asparagus, and Cognac Cream Sauce

When seared, the cocoa-espresso rub gives the lamb a tasty yet slightly bitter "crust". These flavors play well with the robust meat and the creamy polenta. It is highly recommended to cook the lamb to a nice medium rare so as not to "burn" the cocoa-espresso rub, which will make it bitter.

Ingredients

- *6 8-ounce lamb loins*
- *1 pound asparagus*
- *water for cooking*
- *1 cup white polenta*
- *½ stick butter*
- *1 cup milk*
- *1 cup water*
- *½ cup Parmesan cheese*
- *salt and pepper to taste*
- *½ cup espresso powder, finely ground*
- *½ cup cocoa powder*
- *1 tablespoon salt*
- *1 teaspoon black pepper*
- *1 teaspoon chili powder*
- *1 teaspoon granulated garlic*
- *2 ounces cognac*
- *½ cup heavy cream*

Preparation

FOR asparagus, bring pot of water to rolling boil, salt water and blanch asparagus about 3-4 minutes until bright green. Strain and place asparagus in ice bath to stop cooking. Refrigerate and hold.

FOR polenta, add butter to milk and water, bring to simmer, then slowly whisk in white polenta until consistency of loose mashed potatoes. Stir in ½ cup of Parmesan cheese and season to taste with salt and white pepper. Can be made right before cooking lamb and held in warm place.

FOR lamb rub, combine espresso powder, cocoa powder, salt, black pepper, chili powder, and garlic. Mix all together.

PREHEAT oven to 425 degrees.

RUB lamb loins with mixture and sear in sauté pan over high heat. Sear on both sides for about 1 minute, then place in oven for 8 minutes. This will give lamb loins a medium temperature. Give less or more time for your preference. Let lamb rest, in the mean time put asparagus in oven. Then take pan, place back on burner, turn on to high heat and deglaze pan with cognac. It will flame, be careful. When flame burns out, add cream and reduce to sauce consistency. Salt and pepper to taste.

SLICE lamb thinly, assemble on plate with white polenta, asparagus, and finish with sauce.

Serves 6

Wine suggestion: Daedalus Cellars, "Labrynth" Pinot Noir, Oregon 2001

Opal Basil Infused Chocolate Mousse

Ingredients

- 2½ *cups heavy cream*
- 2 *tablespoon chopped opal basil*
- 1 *pound semi-sweet chocolate*
- 6 *ounces egg yolks (approx. 9 yolks)*
- 1 *stick butter, cubed*
- 8 *ounces egg whites (whites of 8-11 eggs, depending on size)*
- ½ *cup sugar*
- 1 *ounce Frangelico, or other hazelnut liqueur*

Preparation

SIMMER ½ cup heavy cream with opal basil for ten minutes. Strain.

OVER a double boiler, melt chocolate, and remove from heat. While stirring, add infused cream, egg yolks (one at a time), and cubed butter.

WHIP egg whites in blender, adding sugar towards end. Whites should look cloud-like.

WHIP 2 cups cream with Frangelico until fluffy. Fold the whipped egg whites, a third at a time, into chocolate. Mix, then repeat with whipped cream.

Serves 12

paley's place

1204 NW 21st Avenue
Portland, OR 97209
503-243-2403

Monday - Thursday
5:30 pm - 10:00 pm
Friday - Saturday
5:30 pm - 11:00 pm
Sunday
5:00 pm - 10:00 pm

Paley's Place

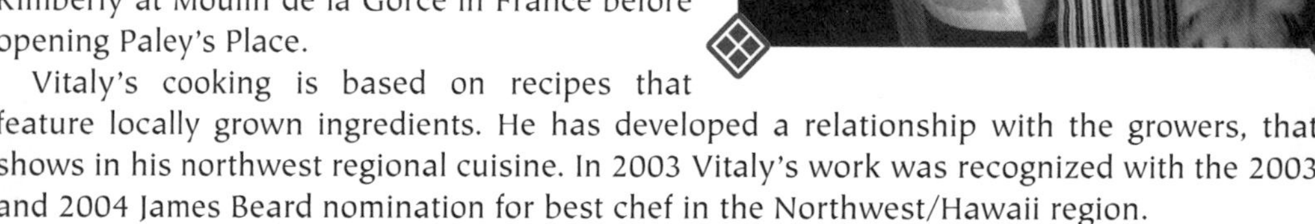

Kimberly and Vitaly Paley came to Portland in 1995 and created a great Northwest bistro with southern French and northern Italian cuisine in a large Victorian house located in Portland's Northwest District. Vitaly, who emigrated to the U.S. from the former Soviet Union, brings an artist's sensitivity to his cooking. Trained as a concert pianist from childhood, he also studied at Julliard School of Music before shifting his creative energies to cooking. He earned a Grand Diploma from the French Culinary Institute in New York. He worked at Union Square Café, Remi and Chanterelle in New York and apprenticed along with his wife Kimberly at Moulin de la Gorce in France before opening Paley's Place.

Vitaly's cooking is based on recipes that feature locally grown ingredients. He has developed a relationship with the growers, that shows in his northwest regional cuisine. In 2003 Vitaly's work was recognized with the 2003 and 2004 James Beard nomination for best chef in the Northwest/Hawaii region.

Kimberly graciously runs the "front of the house" with a dancer's energy: greeting guests, recommending wines and dishes and making sure that everything runs smoothly. Originally from southern California, Kimberly earned a Bachelor of Fine Arts in Performance degree from UCLA. She earned a scholarship to the Graham School of Dance in New York, then gave up her professional dance career to pursue a wine captain's diploma from the Sommelier Society of America. After spending some time working for Windows on the World at the former World Trade Center, she apprenticed at Moulin de la Gorce with her husband, which has helped her build up a great wine list for Paley's Place that features wines from Oregon, Washington and France.

The Paley's hard work and creative cuisine has garnered them a number of accolades.

Gourmet Magazine's Top Tables rated Paley's as a Top 400 Restaurant for two consecutive years. In 1999, Paley's was named Oregonian Restaurant of the Year. And noted wine critic, Robert Parker, rated Paley's as one of his most memorable meals of 2001.

Vitaly says, "My goal and dream, is to be part of the movement to identify what northwest regional cuisine is all about." Vitaly and Kimberly have a great restaurant with sublime food.

Chanterelles

with Potatoes, Olive Oil, Parsley, and Garlic

Ingredients

- 1 *pound chanterelles, cleaned, small buttons preferred*
- ¼ *cup extra virgin olive oil*
- 4 *medium sized yellow flesh potatoes (like Yukon gold), baked, peeled, and coarsely mashed*
- 1 *bunch parsley, chopped*
- 2 *cloves garlic, peeled, and finely chopped*
- *salt and freshly ground black pepper*

Preparation

HEAT some olive oil in a sauté pan over high heat. Add chanterelles to the pan and season them with salt and pepper. Continue cooking, stirring until all the liquid released by the mushrooms has reduced dry. Add potatoes and remaining olive oil. Continue cooking until heated through. Add parsley and garlic. Adjust seasoning if needed. Serve immediately.

Serves 4 as a side dish

Vegetable Stuffed Oregon Morels

with Green Garlic Confit
and Asparagus Cream Ingredients

Ingredients

- 12 *large morels*
- 5 *tablespoons unsalted butter*
- 4 *cups water*
- 1 *medium carrot, chopped*
- 1 *medium onion, chopped*
- ⅔ *cup port wine*
- ½ *cup heavy cream*
- 2 *tablespoons fine, fresh bread crumbs*
- 1 *egg yolk*
- *salt and freshly ground pepper*
- 12 *stalks of thin asparagus, trimmed, peeled, blanched and cut into 2" pieces*
- 1 *tablespoon chopped parsley*
- *Garlic Confit (recipe follows)*

Preparation

WASH morels very gently, but thoroughly, in cold water to rid them of any sand and grit. Cut off stems and set aside.

IN A medium saucepan, bring 4 cups of water to a boil. Add salt, morels, and stems; boil for 1 minute. Drain well. Set morels aside and chop stems very fine. Melt two tablespoons butter in a medium skillet. Add morel stems, carrot, and three-quarters of the chopped onion. Cook slowly until vegetables are soft. Add one-third cup of the port and reduce dry. Stir in two tablespoons of the cream and bread crumbs. Remove from heat and stir in egg yolk. Season with salt and pepper to taste. Transfer the stuffing into a small pastry bag. Pipe the stuffing into the morels. Melt three tablespoons butter in a medium skillet and add morels and remaining chopped onion. Cover and cook over medium heat for 2 minutes. Add remaining port and cream. Cook until the liquid thickens slightly. Remove from heat and set aside.

TO SERVE, reheat the morels in their sauce. Add blanched asparagus and cook just until heated through. Place green garlic confit on bottom of serving bowls. Place 3 morels on top of garlic confit. Arrange 3 asparagus stalks around the plate. Pour the sauce over the morels. Garnish with chopped parsley and serve.

For the Garlic Confit

- 2 *tablespoons unsalted butter*
- 12 *stalks of green garlic, washed and coarsely chopped*
- *salt and pepper to taste*

MELT the butter in a medium size skillet. Add green garlic and cook on medium heat until soft, about 10 to 15 minutes. Season with salt and pepper to taste. Set aside to cool if not using right away.

Serves 4

Paley's Oyster Chowder

Ingredients

- 1 *tablespoon extra virgin olive oil*
- 1 *cup bacon, diced in ¼ inch cubes*
- 3 *stalks leeks (white parts only): washed and cut into half moons*
- 1 *large carrot, peeled and diced into ¼ inch cubes*
- 1 *bottle hard apple cider (if hard cider is not available, use ½ bottle white wine and ½ bottle apple cider)*
- 1 *cup heavy cream*
- 24 *oysters in the shells, shucked, reserving oyster liquid*
- 2 *medium size yellow-fleshed potatoes (like Yukon gold), baked, peeled and diced into ¼ inch cubes*
- 1 *apple, peeled, cored and diced into ¼ inch cubes*
- 1 *tablespoon chopped parsley*
- 1 *tablespoon chopped chives*
- *salt and freshly ground black pepper*

Preparation

IN A soup pot, heat olive oil over medium heat. Add bacon. Stir frequently until the bacon is crispy and brown. Drain the bacon on paper towel and reserve. Pour off some of the bacon fat. Add leeks and carrots and cook until translucent (about 7 minutes). Add apple cider and bring to a boil. Reduce by a quarter or until alcohol has evaporated. Add cream, oysters, oyster liquid, potatoes, and apple. Bring to a boil. Stir in chopped parsley and chives. Season with salt and pepper. Enjoy.

Serves 4

Garden Lettuces with Roasted Beets, Pickled Chanterelles and Caramelized Pears

Ingredients

2 or 3 heads of lettuce, like red oak, butterhead, lola rosa or romaine
7 tablespoons extra virgin olive oil
salt and pepper to taste
Chanterelles (recipe follows)
Beets (recipe follows)
Pears (recipe follows)

Preparation

AT LEAST a couple of days ahead of time prepare the pickled chanterelles. The day of, make the beets and pears. Wash and dry the lettuce.

TO SERVE, place 3 tablespoons of the mushroom pickling liquid in a bowl big enough to hold the lettuce. Add olive oil and stir together well. Add lettuce, mushrooms, beets, and pears. Adjust seasoning with salt and pepper. Serve immediately.

For Chanterelles

1 pound chanterelles
2 cups rice vinegar
1 cup mirin
1 teaspoon coriander
1 teaspoon fennel seed
1 teaspoon cumin seed
2 star anise
1 cinnamon stick
3 cloves
3 bay leaves
3 tablespoons kosher salt

PREHEAT oven to 350 degrees. Place chanterelles on cookie sheet and cook until wilted, about 10-15 minutes. In a non-reactive pot combine vinegar, mirin, and pickling spices, bring to a boil. Turn off heat and let steep for 10 minutes. Place chanterelles in a clean jar or container. Pour the pickling liquid with spices over mushrooms. Cover and place in refrigerator. Mushrooms should be ready within a couple of days.

For Beets

3 Beets
1 tablespoons olive oil
1 teaspoon kosher salt

PLACE beets on a cookie sheet. Drizzle olive oil over them. Season with salt. Place in oven and cook for approximately 1 hour or until fork tender. Let cool, peel, and cut into wedges.

For Pears

- *2 pears, such as crimson scarlet or Bosc*
- *1 tablespoons sugar*
- *¼ cup melted butter*

CUT pears into wedges Place pear wedges onto cookie sheet. Drizzle with melted butter and sprinkle with sugar. Place into oven and cook until golden brown.

Serves 6

Steamed Mussels with Hand-Cut Fries

Ingredients

2 pounds mussels, fresh, scrubbed, unopened
1 tablespoon butter, unsalted
3 cloves garlic, finely minced
1 cup white wine, preferably the wine you will be drinking with the dish
1 bunch parsley, washed, and finely chopped
salt and freshly ground pepper to taste
Aioli (recipe follows)
Fries (recipe follows)
bread for dipping

Preparation

BOTH the mussels and fries should be served immediately. Prepare aioli, then time the fries and mussels to be consumed as soon as cooked. The recipe for the fries is below.

FOR the mussels, start with a shallow, straight-sided saucepan big enough to hold all the shellfish. Combine mussels, butter, garlic, and white wine. Cover and steam for approximately 5 minutes, or until the shells open up. Sprinkle with chopped parsley. Serve immediately with fries and lots of bread for the mussel broth.

For the Aioli

4 garlic cloves, crushed, and peeled
large pinch of coarse sea salt
2 egg yolks
2 cups olive oil
1-2 teaspoons water
2 tablespoons mustard, whole grain

IN A marble mortar with a wooden pestle, pound the salt and garlic to a smooth liquid paste. Add the egg yolks and stir briskly with the pestle until they lighten in color. Begin to add the oil in a tiny trickle. Add to the side of the mortar so that the oil flows gradually into the yolk and garlic mixture, constantly turning the pestle. As the mixture begins to thicken, the flow of oil can be increased to a thick thread, add to the side of the mortar while turning the pestle. Add a teaspoon or two of water to loosen the mixture while turning and continue adding oil until you have obtained the desired quantity and consistency. Stir in the whole grain mustard, cover, and refrigerate until serving.

For the Fries

4 large russet potatoes, scrubbed and cut into ½ inch sticks
oil for frying
salt to taste

FILL a heavy bottom, straight-sided pot half way with oil. Preheat the oil until it reaches 300 degrees as determined by an oil thermometer. Wash and cut potatoes under cold water. Pat them dry and fry in oil until soft, not brown. Drain on paper towels. Turn up the heat until it reaches 375 degrees, as determined by an oil thermometer. Turn the heat down and fry the blanched potatoes until crispy and golden brown. Drain on paper towels. Serve immediately with whole grain mustard aioli.

Serves 4

Cedar Planked Salmon

Ingredients

- *1 3-4 pound filet of salmon, pin boned*
- *1 cedar plank - 1 to 2 inches larger then filet of salmon all the way around*
- *3 tablespoons olive oil for brushing the plank*
- *3 tablespoons olive oil for drizzling over salmon*
- *1 cup brown sugar*
- *¾ cup salt*
- *2 oranges, zested*
- *1 large head of garlic, peeled, chopped very fine*
- *2 large onions peeled, sliced thin*
- *1 cup chiffonade basil*

Preparation

TO FIND cedar planks, shop at a lumber store, and be sure to get untreated cedar shingles.

PREHEAT oven to 450 degrees.

BRUSH one side of the plank with olive oil and place the plank in the oven to get hot and release wood aromas, approximately 15 to 20 minutes. While the plank is heating, up mix salt, brown sugar, and orange zest and spread it generously on both sides of salmon filet. This procedure can be done 1 to 2 hours in advance.

WHEN plank is hot, pull it out of the oven and spread chopped garlic on the plank the length and width of salmon filet. Place salmon on top of garlic purée. Sprinkle the top of salmon with basil and cover generously with sliced onions, and then drizzle with remaining olive oil. Cook in oven for approximately 25 to 30 minutes or until probe thermometer registers at 120 degrees for medium rare.

Serves 10 - 12

Warm Chocolate Soufflé Cake

Ingredients

15 ounces bittersweet chocolate
6 ounces butter
6 eggs
1½ cups sugar
pinch of salt
Honey-Vanilla Ice Cream (recipe follows)

Preparation

PREHEAT oven to 400 degrees. Butter or spray eight 4-ounce ramekins. Melt chocolate pieces and butter in a large bowl over a pot of steaming water. Separate the eggs into two bowls. Whisk the yolks with half the sugar until light in color and sugar is dissolved. Set aside.

WHISK the egg whites with half of the remaining sugar until soft peaks form, then add the rest of the sugar and whisk until firm peaks form. Gently fold yolk mixture into chocolate and butter. Fold egg whites into chocolate mixture in three additions.

POUR batter into ramekins. Bake for 12-14 minutes until set, or refrigerate the unbaked soufflé for a maximum of three days before baking.

SERVE with honey-vanilla ice cream.

For the Honey-Vanilla Ice Cream

1 quart whipping cream
1 vanilla bean
1 pinch of salt
8 egg yolks
½ cup granulated sugar
½ cup of honey

HEAT cream, vanilla (split and remove seeds, place in cream), and salt. Whisk eggs with sugar and honey. Temper warm cream into eggs, return to stove and cook until the mixture coats the back of a spoon. Strain into a stainless steel bowl and chill over ice water bath until cold. Freeze in ice cream machine according to manufacturer's instructions.

Serves 8

Portland Fire Department, Engine 15 - ca.1913.

Papa Haydn

Talk about desserts in Portland and you are likely to hear the name Papa Haydn. This charming restaurant is known for the variety of its delectable desserts.

Portland's first taste of the possibilities came in 1977, when La Patisserie in Portland's Old Town featured a curious dessert called a Dubosch Torte. Created by Jeff and Heidi Van Dyke, the intricate layering of ultra-thin Genoise cake and chocolate butter cream was based on the recipes that Heidi's parents had used in their bakeries in Berlin. Portland had never seen anything like it, and by the end of their first month of production, the couple couldn't keep up with the demand for their growing line of desserts.

It was time to open of a cafe of their own. Papa Haydn East opened in August of 1978.

The 25-seat café, featuring pastries in addition to a limited menu of soups, sandwiches and salads, became an immediate success. A glowing review by Karen Brooks (then of Willamette Week) gave a boost to the popularity of the restaurant, and it was expanded in 1980, and a full kitchen was added.

Heidi's sister, Evelyn Franz, joined the team shortly after opening and took charge of the bakery. The architecturally stunning creations that you see at both Papa Haydn restaurants today are a result of her 25 years of dedication and expertise.

In 1982, Dick and Lori Singer approached Evelyn, Heidi and Jeff about the possibility of opening a second location on Northwest 23rd Avenue. The Singers' vision for the Avenue reflected their instincts about the incredible potential of the area, and Papa Haydn West opened in September of 1983.

Papa Haydn has always prided itself on using fresh and seasonal products, from local producers whenever possible. The restaurant, originally notable for its desserts, has evolved into a fine dining establishment with an excellent wine list, recognized for the last three years with the Award of Excellence from the Wine Spectator. From the first sip of wine to the final tasty morsel, Papa Haydn delights your taste buds.

Chèvre Paté

This appetizer has been on our menu since we opened our doors. It is a nice addition to any cocktail buffet, and also makes a terrific lunch entrée when served with a simple green salad. Leftovers will keep when well wrapped and stored in the refrigerator for up to five days.

Ingredients

- *10½ ounces Montrachet cheese*
- *10½ ounces feta cheese*
- *2 cloves garlic*
- *3 eggs, separated*
- *⅜ cup sun dried tomatoes, minced*
- *18 pimento-stuffed green olives*
- *grape leaves for lining pan*

Preparation

PREHEAT oven to 350 degrees. Line a 4½" x 10" loaf pan with plastic wrap.

LINE sides and bottom of loaf pan with overlapping grape leaves.

PUT cheeses, garlic and egg yolks in the bowl of a food processor and process until smooth. Transfer to a large mixing bowl.

BEAT egg whites until stiff and gently fold into cheese mixture.

FILL pan ⅓ full with cheese mixture and add a layer of green olives. Add 1/3 more of the mixture; then a layer of the sun dried tomatoes; top with the remainder of the cheese mixture.

COVER pan with foil. Make three slits in the foil with a sharp knife. Place in a large baking dish and fill the dish with boiling water. Bake for approximately one hour or until toothpick comes out clean. Remove and let cool. Cut to preferred thickness and serve as desired, with bread or mixed greens, for example.

Serves 6-8, as an appetizer

Wine suggestion: We like to pair this up with a grassy, crisp Sauvignon Blanc, like the 2002 from Pepi Vineyards.

Caesar Salad

A classic. Serve as is or top with a grilled chicken breast, salmon filet, or grilled flank steak.

Ingredients

- 2 *medium heads romaine*
- ⅛ *cup pasteurized egg yolks*
- 3 *cloves garlic, minced*
- 4 *anchovy filets, minced*
- ½ *tablespoon freshly cracked black pepper*
- 1 *teaspoon Worcestershire sauce*
- 1 *teaspoon Dijon mustard*
- 1 *tablespoon lime juice*
- 1 *cup olive oil*
- *Parmigiano-Reggiano cheese*
- *Croutons (recipe follows)*

Preparation

WASH the lettuce and dry well. Tear in to pieces and place in a salad bowl.

WHISK together egg yolks, garlic, anchovies, pepper, Worcestershire sauce, Dijon mustard, and lime juice, or pulse in a blender until smooth. Gradually drizzle in the olive oil, whisking or blending to incorporate.

TOSS the salad well with one half cup of the dressing and the croutons, adding more dressing as needed. Shave the cheese over the salad and serve.

ANY leftover dressing will keep in the refrigerator for up to 5 days.

For the Croutons

- ½ *crusty baguette*
- 2 *peeled cloves of garlic*

CUT or tear the bread into bite-sized pieces. Rub all sides with the garlic. Brush lightly with olive oil, spread on a sheet pan and toast until golden, about six minutes.

Serves 6

Wine suggestion: This matches nicely with a Pinot Blanc from Alsace; we especially like the 2001 from Les Pierres Chaudes.

Garlic-Horseradish Mashed Potatoes

These have been on the menu at our sister restaurant, Jo Bar and Rotisserie, since its inception, and this has become our most requested recipe. Do not substitute regular garlic for the elephant garlic; its mellowness is the key to the desired results.

Ingredients

2 pounds russet potatoes, peeled and cut into 1" cubes
3 tablespoons unsalted butter
1 tablespoon grated horseradish
2 tablespoons heavy cream
2 teaspoons kosher salt
1½ teaspoons ground white pepper
Roasted Garlic Puree (recipe follows)

Preparation

BOIL potatoes in salted water until fork-tender. Drain and place potatoes in a large mixing bowl. Add the other ingredients, along with 2 tablespoons of the roasted garlic puree, and mash with a whisk or masher until you reach the desired consistency. Serve immediately.

For the Roasted Garlic Puree

2 cloves elephant garlic
salt and pepper

DRIZZLE cloves with olive oil. Season with salt and pepper. Roast at 350 degrees until tender. Cool. Squeeze garlic out of the skin and whip into puree with a whisk.

Serves 4

Bresaola Steak

Traditional bresaola is rubbed with spices and air-dried, thinly sliced and served at room temperature. We think the spice rub works equally well with a grilled steak. Serve with our Garlic Horseradish Mashed Potatoes (recipe included) and a simple grilled vegetable. We like a nice, spicy red wine with this, to mirror the ingredients in the rub.

Ingredients

- 4 *8-ounce tenderloin steaks*
- 1¼ *tablespoons brown sugar*
- ½ *tablespoon freshly ground pepper*
- ½ *teaspoon dried thyme*
- ¼ *teaspoon ground ginger*
- ¼ *teaspoon ground allspice*
- ¼ *teaspoon ground coriander*
- ¼ *teaspoon ground cloves*
- 1½ *tablespoons crushed cardamom seeds*
- 1½ *tablespoons salt*
- *Horseradish Cream (recipe follows)*

Preparation

RUB the filet with brown sugar and all of the spices except for the salt. Place in a non-corrosive dish and cover with foil. Refrigerate for 2 days, turning the meat once a day. Then rub the filet with the salt and refrigerate for one more day. Brush with oil and grill to order. Serve with Horseradish Cream.

For the Horseradish Cream

- 3-4 *tablespoons grated horseradish*
- 3-4 *tablespoons white vinegar*
- ¾ *cup sour cream*
- ¼ *cup heavy cream*
- ½ *teaspoon salt*
- *freshly ground pepper to taste*
- 1½ *tablespoons chopped fresh dill*

MIX all ingredients together and chill.

Serves 4

Wine suggestion: Try this with the 2001 Syrah from Terre Rouge.

Boccone Dolce

Papa Haydn is known for their fabulous desserts. Here's a spectacular one! (Boccone Dolce means "sweet mouthful.")

Ingredients

1¼ cups fresh egg whites
2 cups sugar
4-6 ounces chocolate
6 cups heavy whipping cream
3-4 cups mixed berries, cut
edible flowers and mint

Preparation

PREHEAT oven to 200 degrees. Whip egg whites at a high speed to stiff peaks. Turn speed to medium and start adding sugar, ¼ cup at a time, over a 20-minute period.

WHILE egg whites are whipping, prepare pans. On parchment paper, trace 3 nine-inch circles. Turn parchment over on to cookie sheets (the pen or marker used to trace circles will color the meringue otherwise). When meringue is finished being whipped, it should be thick and have a glossy appearance. Use a rubber spatula and divide meringue between the three circles. Spread with a metal spatula.

BAKE at 200 degrees for four hours. Remove from oven and cool. Store in air-tight container until ready to use. (When ready to use, if meringue feels soft or sticky to the touch, you can re-crisp in a 200 degree oven for 20 minutes.)

TO ASSEMBLE, melt chocolate and whip cream. Reserve a portion of the whipped cream and berries for garnish. Place one layer of meringue on a serving plate and drizzle with chocolate. Spread a third of the whipped cream on next, then sprinkle a layer of mixed berries. Put a little bit of whipped cream on top to help the next layer of meringue adhere. Repeat two more times, ending with meringue on top. Drizzle with chocolate. Decorate with reserved whipped cream, berries, edible flowers, and mint.

Serves 12

Saxer Brewery - ca. 1860.
First brewery in Portland.

Tuscany Grill

811 NW 21st Ave.
Portland, OR 97209
503-243-2757
www.tuscanygrill.com

Monday –Thursday
4:30 pm – 10:00 pm
Friday and Saturday
4:30 pm – 11:00 pm
Sunday
5:00 pm – 10:00 pm

Tuscany Grill

Walking into the Tuscany Grill is like walking into a family Italian kitchen. The warm walls and cozy atmosphere make you feel right at home. Colleen Mendola, one of the owners, will likely greet you with a warm smile. She and her husband, Chef Pat, moved to Portland in 1995 and shortly after opened the Tuscany Grill. They met at the Marina Café in New York where Colleen was a server and Pat was the executive chef. After their marriage they opened their first restaurant Patricio in Staten Island, which received many favorable articles in the New York city press. After a visit to her sister in Portland, Colleen convinced Pat to sell their restaurant and move to Portland.

Since opening, the Tuscany Grill has received a number of strong accolades. It has ranked among City Search's Top 100 list, and in 2003 was named by City Search as the Best Italian Restaurant. At the 2003 "Taste of the Nation", Tuscany Grill was named one of "7 Gems". While Pat created the essence of the restaurant's fare, the current Chef, Paul De Carli, has added his touch to the menu also. The Pappardelle con Coniglio (Rabbit) is a succulent dish with the rabbit slowly braised in wine with carrots, onions and mushrooms and tossed with homemade pasta. Another house favorite is their Braised Lamb Shanks with Risotto Milanese, Fennel and Chive Gremolata. Their wine cellar has between 3,000-3,500 bottles, dating back to 1985. The great wine list features Italian wines, including many wines not found on other wine lists.

Colleen and Pat love the restaurant business. According to Colleen, "We always said that we wanted to make our restaurant an extension of our own dining room at home. We want people to visit us at the Tuscany Grill because we can't fit them all around our table at home. Over the years we have made some wonderful friends and customers." This terrific Tuscany restaurant serves delicious food and wine in a warm friendly setting; a dining experience that you will want to repeat often.

Sicilian Pork Chops

When he was a young boy, Pat's father moved from Sicily to New York with his parents. This recipe has been passed down for generations in the Mendola family, and has been on our menu from day one. It is the only item that remains with every menu change.

Ingredients

- 4 *thick center-cut pork chops (we prefer ones with the bone in)*
- 2 *cups bread crumbs*
- ½ *cup grated cheese (we use Pecorino Romano)*
- 6 *cloves of garlic, smashed and chopped fine*
- ½ *teaspoon crushed red pepper*
- 2 *tablespoons Italian parsley, chopped fine*
- 4-6 *basil leaves chopped fine*
- ½ *small sprig of rosemary, cleaned and chopped*
- *extra virgin olive oil*
- *butter*
- *small jar of pepperoncinis, juice reserved*
- 2 *tablespoons butter*
- *rosemary sprigs for garnish.*

Preparation

COMBINE the bread crumbs, grated cheese, garlic, red pepper, Italian parsley, basil leaves, and rosemary together. Put small amount of olive oil in a bowl or dish, soak pork chops and then dredge in bread crumb mixture. Place coated chops on cutting board and press firmly to make sure the bread crumbs are soaked in oil.

ARRANGE chops in shallow baking dish, add one to two pepperoncini peppers per chop in pan, and bake at 450 degrees for 15 minutes.

TURN chops over (should be golden brown) and add ½ to 1 cup of the pepperoncini peppers to pan. Return to oven and cook through, approximately 10 minutes.

TO MAKE the sauce, use the juices in the baking pan and mount butter over medium heat.

SERVE sauce around and over chops. Garnish with sprigs of rosemary.

Serves 4

Wine Suggestion: a glass of Nero D'Avola, a Sicilian varietal.

Braised Lamb Shanks

with Risotto Milanese, Fennel and Chive Gremolata

Ingredients

- *4 large, meaty lamb shanks*
- *salt and pepper*
- *6 tablespoons olive oil*
- *1 medium carrot, chopped into ¼ inch coins*
- *1 large yellow onion, sliced*
- *2 bulbs fennel, sliced*
- *8 garlic cloves, whole*
- *2 tablespoon fresh chopped rosemary*
- *2 cups red wine*
- *2 cups beef stock*
- *16 ounce can plum tomatoes*
- *½ cup balsamic vinegar*
- *Risotto Milanese (recipe follows)*
- *Fennel and Chive Gremolata (recipe follows)*

Preparation

ONE day prior to cooking, rinse and dry shanks and season liberally with salt and pepper.

ON DAY of, preheat oven to 375 degrees. In a heavy bottom-braising pan, heat olive oil over medium/high heat until just smoking. Add shanks and sear until golden brown on all sides, approximately 15 minutes. Remove shanks and set aside.

ADD carrot, onion, fennel, garlic, and rosemary to the pan. Cook until soft, about 8-10 minutes. Add the wine, beef stock, tomatoes, and balsamic vinegar and bring to a boil. Return shanks to pan, cover tightly, and place in oven for 1½ to 2 hours or until fork tender. Remove and serve over risotto Milanese and top with fennel and chive gremolata.

For the Risotto Milanese

- *¼ cup olive oil*
- *1 medium yellow onion, quartered and diced*
- *2 cups Carnaroli rice*
- *1 teaspoon saffron threads*
- *4 cups chicken stock, hot*
- *4 tablespoon butter*
- *½ cup freshly grated Parmigiano-Reggiano*

IN A 12-14 inch skillet, heat olive oil over medium heat. Add onion and cook until soft and translucent, do not brown. Add rice and saffron threads, stir with a wooden spoon until opaque and toasted, about 3-4 minutes. Add 4 six-ounce ladles of stock and cook, stirring until it is absorbed. Continue to add stock a ladle at a time, waiting until it's absorbed before adding more. Cook the rice until tender and creamy, yet still a little al dente. Add butter and cheese and stir until well blended.

For the Fennel and Chive Gremolata

- ¼ *cup Italian parsley, finely chopped*
- ¼ *cup chives, finely chopped*
- ¼ *cup fennel fronds, finely chopped*
- 2 *clove garlic, peeled and finely chopped*
- *zest of one lemon*

MIX all ingredients until well incorporated. Set aside until ready to serve

Serves 4

Pappardelle con Coniglio (Rabbit)

This is a favorite main dish. People are often afraid to try rabbit, but once convinced, it immediately becomes a favorite.

Ingredients

- *2 whole rabbits (or chicken)*
- *flour for dredging*
- *salt and pepper to taste*
- *olive oil for browning*
- *1 yellow onion, julienned*
- *2 carrots, cut on a bias*
- *3 cups shiitake mushrooms, sliced*
- *½ cup roasted garlic*
- *1 tablespoon fresh rosemary, finely chopped*
- *2 cups dry red wine*
- *4 cups beef stock (substitute chicken stock if using chicken instead of rabbit)*
- *4 cups tomato sauce*
- *Pappardelle (recipe follows)*

Preparation

TO MAKE the rabbit ragu, begin by washing the rabbit thoroughly. Cut into quarters, removing the loins. Carefully remove the silver skin from the loins. Season rabbit quarters and loins with salt and pepper. Dredge with flour. Brown rabbit in a braising pan with olive oil at medium high heat. Remove rabbit from pan. Add onion, carrot, mushrooms, and garlic to pan and sauté until tender. Add rosemary and sauté an additional 2 minutes. Deglaze pan with red wine. Add stock and tomato sauce. Bring all to a boil. Cover and place in oven at 350 degrees for approximately 2 hours or until meat easily separates from the bone.

CAREFULLY remove all bones from the rabbit pieces and shred any larger pieces of meat. Return pan to stove and bring mixture to a simmer. Let mixture reduce until thickened. Adjust seasoning with salt and pepper.

JUST prior to serving, boil pappardelle in six quarts of salted water for about 3 to 4 minutes or until al dente. Strain and toss with ragu.

For the Pappardelle

- *1¼ pounds flour*
- *11 egg yolks*
- *1 tablespoon extra virgin olive oil*
- *¼ cup water*
- *6 quarts salted water*

PLACE the flour in a mound on a clean work surface. Make a well in the center. Lightly beat the yolks with the olive oil and pour into the well of the flour. Stir with a fork to combine. Slowly pour the water over the mixture and stir again until it begins to form a mass. Alternately squeeze and push down on the dough to gather it together. Continually pull any loose pieces of dough back into the mass.

WHEN the dough feels tacky and fully incorporated, knead it for 4 to 5 minutes, or until it loses its surface moisture, is a uniform color, and springs back when depressed. Wrap dough in plastic for one hour.

CUT dough into quarters. Beginning with one of the quarters, roll dough on a lightly floured surface, with rolling pin to approximately 1/16 of an inch in thickness. Fold dough over on itself, and roll out to 1/16 inch again. Repeat this process one more time in order to fully work the dough. Once it is rolled flat for the final time, cut into ½-inch pasta ribbons. Dust lightly with flour to prevent from sticking until ready to cook. Repeat with remaining dough.

Serves 4–6

Wine suggestion: An Italian Brunello or Rosso di Montalcino, such as a 1997 Martinozzi Brunello di Montalcino.

Pappardelle con Coniglio (Rabbit)

Panna Cotta

This is a light, creamy dessert that we often infuse with additional flavors. Right now we are serving a fennel panna cotta on our dessert menu.

Ingredients

- 1 *quart cream*
- 1 *vanilla bean*
- ½ *cup sugar*
- 3½ *gelatin sheets, softened in cold water*
- *fresh berries, as desired*

Preparation

ADD cream, vanilla bean, and sugar to a pot. Heat to steam. Squeeze all excess water out of gelatin. Whisk gelatin into hot liquid and ladle liquid into six 6-ounce ramekins. Refrigerate for 2 to 3 hours. Serve this dessert in the summer with fresh berries.

Serves 6

1221 NW 21st Ave.
Portland, OR 97209
503-248-9663
www.wildwoodrestaurant.com

Monday – Sunday
11:30 am - 2:30 pm
Sunday
Family Style Supper
5:00 pm – 9:00 pm
Monday – Thursday
5:30 pm - 9 pm
Friday – Saturday
5:30 pm – 10:00 pm

Wildwood Restaurant & Bar

The pale earth-toned walls and wood floors are the perfect backdrop for the center stage of this restaurant. When you walk through the front door, your eye immediately goes to the Chef's Counter, a terrazzo counter set up around the open kitchen. If you wish to view the magic of Cory Schreiber's cooking, these are the best seats in the house. Or, if a more intimate dinner is desired, enjoy one of the sumptuous booths. Either way, you are in for a culinary treat that has been a mainstay of the Portland restaurant scene for over 10 years.

Cory Schreiber, the Executive Chef of Wildwood, is a fifth-generation Oregonian. His family has been involved in the Pacific Northwest oyster business since the mid-1800s. He got his start in the restaurant business by washing dishes at his family's restaurant, Dan & Louis Oyster Bar. He served his apprenticeship at the Benson Hotel, and then went on to top restaurants throughout the U.S. to further hone his culinary skills. Cory is the winner of the 1998 James Beard Award as Best Chef Northwest. He is also known for writing "the book" on northwest cooking: "Wildwood - Cooking From the Source in the Pacific Northwest".

The cooking philosophy at Wildwood is epitomized in the title of the book. Wildwood restaurant supports local farms that practice environmentally sound agriculture and sustainable farming. The cuisine is elegant but unfussy. The menu changes seasonally to use the wonderful abundance of the local farmers to its best advantage. Cory and his staff choose the freshest ingredients; building dishes around unique combinations that blend their flavors in just the right way. A typical evening's menu might include Cattail Creek Lamb Mixed Grill served on a bed of creamed cabbage and potatoes with balsamic roasted nectarine and wilted spinach, Grilled Albacore Tuna on a pan braise of tomatoes and fennel with mussels, clams, and garlic. Save room for some fabulous desserts, like Blackberry, Blueberry and Nectarine Pandowdy with vanilla bean ice cream.

The extensive wine list features Oregon, Washington and California wines. Wildwood's culinary philosophy follows through in the wine selections. The list features many artisan producers and is updated weekly to complement the changing seasonal food menu. However, Wildwood features the Oregon Pinot Noir year round, having 15 to 20 selections available at all times.

Marinated Tomato Salad

with Fennel, Carrots and Arugula

Every growing season, I subscribe to Gathering Together Farm Community Supported Agriculture (CSA) program and receive a box of produce weekly. This gets money into the farmer's business when they need it the most, as they start up the farm for another season. The ingredients in this salad all arrive in peak flavor with splendid colors in mid-summer and are great when tossed together raw in a salad. I recommend the Gathering Together Farm box to anyone looking for a constant supply of summer produce. You can enjoy the surprise of finding something different each week and letting the farmer do the shopping for you!
~Cory Schreiber

Ingredients

- ¼ *cup extra virgin olive oil*
- 2 *tablespoons red wine vinegar*
- ¼ *cup whole cilantro leaves*
- 1 *teaspoon coriander seeds, toasted and ground or cracked with the broad side of a knife*
- 6 *ripe tomatoes, any variety, cut in half, core removed and cut into sixths or eighths, depending on their size*
- 1 *bulb fennel, trimmed, cut in half, core removed and thinly sliced crosswise*
- 1 *small red onion, peeled and thinly sliced crosswise*
- 1 *carrot, peeled and thinly sliced at an angle*
- 8 *ounces of young, tender arugula leaves*
- 1 *teaspoon salt*
- ½ *teaspoon freshly ground black pepper*

Preparation

IN A small bowl, whisk together the oil, vinegar, cilantro leaves and coriander seeds. Set aside.

IN A medium bowl, combine the tomatoes, sliced fennel, red onion, and carrot. Toss with the vinaigrette and marinate for one hour.

JUST before serving, toss in the arugula, salt and pepper.

SPOON onto plates or bowls and serve.

Serves 4

Indianhead Farm Elephant Garlic Paste

Indianhead Farm is a great example of how food purchasing is networked through Portland chefs. Having dinner at a local restaurant, I noticed the wonderful elephant garlic the chef used. I asked which farm supplied it, and Bill Chambers' name came up. I called Bill and next thing I knew his beautiful garlic arrived at Wildwood. This Oregon State Fair Blue Ribbon product comes beautifully tied in red woven nets and is impeccable in quality and flavor. With product this good, the best thing to do is let it stand on its own. Indianhead Farm sells its elephant garlic and other produce at the Portland Farmers Market.
~Cory Schreiber

Ingredients

- 6 *cloves of elephant garlic, peeled*
- *water to cover*
- ⅓ *cup olive oil*
- 1 *teaspoon chopped fresh rosemary*
- 1 *tablespoon lemon zest*
- 1 *tablespoon freshly squeezed lemon juice*
- 1 *teaspoon salt*
- 1 *teaspoon freshly ground black pepper*

Preparation

PLACE the peeled garlic cloves into a stainless steel pot and cover with water. (Use a stainless steel pot to avoid discoloration.) Bring to a boil; reduce the heat and let simmer for three minutes. Strain the garlic cloves and rinse with cold water. Repeat this blanching process two more times, or until the garlic cloves are soft. Let cool for a few minutes, then place garlic into a mortar or a large bowl.

ADD the olive oil, rosemary, lemon juice, lemon zest, salt and freshly ground black pepper. Using the pestle or a large spoon, slowly smash the garlic cloves into a coarse paste.

USE this paste as a topping for a pizza with Juniper Grove Goat Cheese, or spread it on a toasted baguette and melt a slice of Oregon Gourmet Camembert Cheese on top.

Asparagus on a Salad of Spring Onions and Radishes

with Dungeness Crab Mayonnaise

Candace and Warwick Smith are great examples of single product-focus farmers. They built a house in Parkdale in the shadow of Mt. Hood with a view of Cooper Spur, and inherited an asparagus farm alongside beautiful apple orchards. Who would have known that great asparagus grows at 2,500 feet? If you can find their impeccable product in its short, six-week growing period, this salad will highlight the light grassy tones and full-bodied texture of the asparagus with the natural pairing of Oregon's favorite crabmeat.
~Cory Schreiber

Ingredients

- 16 *asparagus spears, peeled and trimmed*
- ¾ *cup extra virgin olive oil*
- 2 *teaspoons salt*
- 2 *teaspoons freshly ground black pepper*
- 3 *medium spring onions, thinly sliced into rings*
- 6 *radishes, thinly sliced*
- ¼ *cup Chardonnay vinegar*
- 2 *tablespoons lemon zest*
- 1 *teaspoon fresh picked thyme leaves*
- ¼ *pound fresh lump Dungeness crab meat*
- 1 *tablespoon freshly squeezed lemon juice*
- 2 *tablespoons minced fresh flat-leaf parsley*
- ¾ *cup prepared mayonnaise*

Preparation

PLACE the asparagus spears in a large sauté pan half-filled with water. Add ¼ cup of the olive oil, 1 teaspoon salt and 1 teaspoon pepper; simmer together until the asparagus is tender, about 5 minutes. Remove the asparagus from the water and set aside.

IN A medium bowl, combine the onions, radishes, vinegar, remaining olive oil, lemon zest, thyme, 1 teaspoon salt and 1 teaspoon pepper. Toss to coat. Season to taste and let the salad marinate for 1 hour.

IN A separate small bowl, combine the crab, lemon juice, parsley, and mayonnaise. Set aside.

TO SERVE, spoon marinated vegetables onto chilled salad plates. Lay 4 asparagus spears on top of the salad and top with the crab and parsley.

Serves 4

Caramel Roasted Anjou Pear French Tart

Oregonians know that Hood River is the Pear Capital of the World. I have located there the most flavorful pears from Apeasay Farms, an organic farm run by North Chetham. His Bosc pears combine a nice firmness for roasting with a buttery texture that brings the pear's sugar to full ripeness, and a pleasant nose. I usually have this tart at six in the morning, if I'm lucky enough to find a slice or two left over from the previous night's service. Either fresh from the oven or the next day, the pears make the difference.
~Cory Schreiber

Ingredients

- *1 pound puff pastry, thawed*
- *7 ripe Anjou pears, peeled, halved and cored*
- *½ cup sugar, plus extra for sprinkling over tart*
- *1 teaspoon vanilla extract*
- *⅛ teaspoon salt*
- *¼ teaspoon ground cinnamon*
- *1 medium egg, beaten*

Preparation

PREHEAT the oven to 400 degrees.

IN A medium bowl, toss the pears with sugar, vanilla extract, salt, and cinnamon. Place on a parchment lined baking sheet; and roast, stirring occasionally, until sugar is syrupy and golden brown and most of the liquid has evaporated. This will take 20-30 minutes. Remove from the oven and set aside to cool.

ON A floured surface, divide puff pastry dough into two pieces. Roll one piece into a 10-inch circle. Place this dough on a parchment lined baking sheet. Roll the second piece of puff pastry into a 12-inch circle. Refrigerate both pieces of pastry for 30 minutes.

PLACE the roasted, cooled pears evenly onto the 10-inch circle of puff pastry, leaving a 1-inch border around the edge of the pastry. Brush the border of the pastry with the beaten egg. Place the 12-inch round of pastry over the pears and press the two pieces of pastry together around the border. Tuck the excess dough under the tart and flute the edge of the crust using the tines of a fork. Refrigerate for 10 minutes.

BRUSH the tart with the remaining beaten egg and sprinkle with sugar. Cut decorative vents into the center top of tart.

BAKE at 400 degrees for 20 -30 minutes, rotating the pan to ensure even baking. The tart should be a dark, caramel brown color. Serve warm with ice cream or whipped cream. Tart is best served within a few hours of baking.

Serves 6–8

Plainfield's Mayur

851 SW 21st
Portland, OR 97205
503-223-2995
www.plainfields.com

Seven nights a week
From 5:30 pm until close

Plainfield's Mayur

Portland boasts the only Indian restaurant in the world that has received the Wine Spectator's Best of Award of Excellence as well as the only one in the country to receive the Top Table Award from Gourmet Magazine.

In 1977, Rich Plainfield opened his restaurant on the corner of NW 21st and Kearney. In 1986, he moved it to its current location, in the exquisitely beautiful historic mansion overlooking the city. The word "mayur" is derived from the ancient Sanskrit word for peacock, a perfectly apropos word for both the setting and the fine food.

The 1901 Victorian mansion has been decorated in the style of the time, with Queen Anne tables and chairs, Royal Dalton china, full silver service and European crystal. On winter evenings, you will find a welcoming fire in the fireplace. The genteel atmosphere is furthered by the soft classical Indian music playing in the background. Outside, there is a large garden patio, complete with a Victorian gazebo. While the service is formal, a relaxed informal atmosphere is encouraged.

The cuisine reflects thousands of years of culinary tradition. Indian cuisine is based on the exotic flavors of the masalas that are used in the various dishes. Masalas are blends of spices that are individually roasted, ground, and then blended together in different combinations. Each masala adds a different flavor to a dish. Most masalas are family traditions and are handed down from generation to generation, and are often closely guarded. It is a mistake to assume that this heavy use of spices creates an overly hot cuisine. Plainfield's Mayur uses the hot spices conservatively, preferring to serve a tray of condiments so that the individual diner can add his or her own personal heat level to the dishes. One of the focal points of the restaurant is the Tandoori show kitchen. The ancient method of cooking in high heat with large clay pots is demonstrated for you. The 1000-degree heat of the oven imparts a mellow smokiness to the meats that are baked in this manner.

The extensive menu is a delight to read, offering not only a comprehensive explanation of each dish, but many describe the history of the dish also. The restaurant's wine menu is another bit of history. Featuring a 4,000-bottle inventory, it spans over two centuries with some vintages dating back to the late 1700's. The restaurant boasts that it contains the most extensive collection of Madeira in the country, with vintages from every decade over the past 200 years. No need to feel intimidated by this extensive list, there are choices for every palate and every wallet, making a perfect complement to a delightful and exotic meal.

Bread Khichadi

(Spicy Indian stuffing)

Here is an Indian dish that will remind you of your mother's famous stuffing, but this one you eat for breakfast!

Ingredients

- *⅓ cup oil*
- *½ teaspoon mustard seeds*
- *1 teaspoon turmeric*
- *2 green chilies, sliced thin*
- *½ cup peanuts*
- *1 cup diced onions*
- *½ cup diced tomatoes*
- *½ cup green peas*
- *1 teaspoon salt*
- *1 tablespoon sugar*
- *8 cups cubed bread*
- *coconut (for garnish)*
- *coriander (for garnish)*

Preparation

HEAT the oil in a pan to medium high heat. When the oil is hot, add mustard seeds, then turmeric and chilies. Add the peanuts and brown slightly. Add onions and cook until soft. Add tomatoes, peas, salt, sugar, and bread. Toss until all the bread is coated. Cover and steam three minutes. Toss again and cover and cook for three more minutes. You can either serve this soft or cook more until crisp. Garnish with coconut and coriander. Goes well with yogurt and lemon.

Serves 4

Masala Dosa

(Vegan)

This classic South Indian Breakfast / Snack of lentil and rice pancakes with spicy potato filling is nutritious, inexpensive and easy to make. The batter can be stored in the refrigerator for over a week, so you can make dosa in a matter of minutes.

Ingredients

1 cup split white urid daal
2 cups rice, uncooked
2 teaspoons salt
¾ cup water
Filling (recipe follows)

Preparation

WASH rice and daal in separate bowls. Cover with cold water and let it soak at room temperature for 8 - 10 hours. Blend rice with half of the water to paste. Remove it in a deep bowl. Next blend daal with remaining water until creamy.

COMBINE batters, cover, and let them sit for 10-12 hours in a warm place to ferment. Heat a heavy skillet (preferably non-stick) over medium heat until hot. Pour ½ cup of batter in center of skillet and with the back of the ladle, starting from the center, spread the batter out very thin, using a circular motion. Dribble a little oil around edges and cook until crisp.

MAKE filling, place in center and roll up.

For the Filling

4 tablespoon oil
1 teaspoon mustard seeds
1 teaspoon turmeric
2 green chilies, sliced
1 onion, diced
1 teaspoon salt
1 pound potatoes, peeled, cubed, cooked
½ cup fresh cilantro, chopped

HEAT oil in skillet until hot. Add mustard seeds. They will pop. Immediately add turmeric and chilies. Next, add onions and salt and cook till onions are translucent. Add potatoes and cook 5 minutes. Fold in cilantro leaves.

Serves 4-6

Potato Khis

(Indian hash browns)

After you make this dish, hash browns will never be the same. It is traditionally served for breakfast fried crisp and garnished with chopped coriander leaves and accompanied by fresh yogurt and lemon wedges.

Ingredients

- *4 potatoes*
- *2 teaspoons salt*
- *1 tablespoon sugar*
- *½ cup finely ground peanuts*
- *⅓ cup oil*
- *1 teaspoon cumin seeds*
- *1 or 2 green chilies, sliced fine*
- *fresh chopped coriander (for garnish)*
- *grated coconut (for garnish)*

Preparation

PAR-BOIL the potatoes, then peel and grate them. Mix grated potatoes, salt, sugar, and ground peanuts. Heat oil until hot, add cumin seeds, and fry for five seconds. Add sliced chilies and fry for ten seconds. Add potato mixture and stir. Cover and cook five minutes on medium heat. Uncover, stir, and fry until crisp. Garnish with fresh chopped coriander and grated coconut.

Serves 4

Upmaa

(Spicy cream of wheat)

This dish is traditionally served for breakfast or with afternoon tea. It is very nutritious and low fat and quick to make. Try it tomorrow for breakfast!

Ingredients

- *1 cup cream of wheat*
- *1 tablespoon oil*
- *1 teaspoon cumin seeds*
- *2 dried red chilies (optional)*
- *½ cup peanuts*
- *1 teaspoon salt*
- *¾ cup onions, finely diced*
- *2-3 cups boiling water*
- *chopped coriander leaves (optional, for garnish)*
- *plain yogurt (optional, for garnish)*

Preparation

ROAST the cream of wheat in a pan until it turns a slightly yellow-brown. Remove from pan and set aside. Heat oil in pan, add cumin and chilies. Fry five to ten seconds. Then add peanuts, salt, and onions. Cook until onions are golden brown. Add the roasted cream of wheat and 2 cups of boiling water. The cream of wheat will absorb the water. Stir, turn down the heat to med-low, cover and cook for five minutes until the cream of wheat feels soft to the touch and tastes "done". Additional water, up to 1 cup, may have to be added before the cream of wheat is completely cooked. Garnish with chopped coriander leaves and serve with plain yogurt.

Serves 4

Pumpkin Raita

Here is a great side dish that has lots of flavor. You can use any type of winter squash for this.

Ingredients

- 3 *pounds pumpkin*
- ¼ *cup oil*
- ½ *teaspoon mustard seeds*
- 1 *teaspoon turmeric*
- 2 *green chilies, sliced*
- 1½ *teaspoons salt*
- 2 *teaspoons sugar*
- 1 *cup yogurt*
- ½ *cup sour cream*
- *chopped coriander leaves*

Preparation

BAKE pumpkin at 350 degrees until cooked but firm, about 30 minutes. Peel and coarsely mash. Heat oil on medium high heat in a pan. When the oil is hot, add mustard seeds, then turmeric, and then chilies. Add mashed pumpkin and mix together. Remove to mixing bowl. Add salt, sugar, yogurt, and sour cream. Mix and chill. Garnish with chopped coriander leaves.

Serves 4

Masala Murgh with Naan Bread

(Chicken in spices)

This classic Indian chicken dish is great over rice or with traditional Naan bread (recipe follows). The Naan bread is a North Indian staple, traditionally cooked in large earthen pots called tandoors. This rendition may be baked in your home oven.

Ingredients

- 1 *teaspoon saffron threads*
- 2 *tablespoons hot water*
- 3½ *pounds chicken pieces*
- 3 *cloves garlic, mashed*
- 1½ *teaspoons salt*
- 1 *inch piece ginger, grated*
- ½ *teaspoon ground turmeric*
- 4 *tablespoons yogurt*
- ½ *teaspoon cayenne pepper*
- 1 *teaspoon garam masala*
- 3 *tablespoons oil*
- 8 *eggs, boiled and peeled*
- *Cooking Sauce (recipe follows)*
- *Naan Bread (recipe follows)*

Preparation

SOAK saffron threads in the hot water. Set aside. Blend garlic, salt, ginger, ground turmeric, yogurt, cayenne pepper, and garam masala together in a blender, then rub the mixture on the chicken pieces. Place in a bowl, cover, and let sit at room temperature for 2 hours. Make cooking sauce while chicken marinates.

REMOVE chicken from bowl and heat oil in a large skillet and cook chicken pieces to seal in the juices. They will not brown. Add the rest of the marinade and the cooking sauce paste from the blender. Taste for salt. Cover and simmer about 35 minutes. Add boiled eggs and cook 10 minutes more. Place chicken and sauce on a large platter. Arrange eggs around it and sprinkle with chopped coriander leaves and fresh grated coconut. Goes well with hot naan bread and steamed basmati rice.

For the Cooking Sauce

- 5 *tablespoons oil*
- 3 *onions diced*
- 1 *inch ginger, grated*
- 4 *tablespoons blanched almonds, chopped*
- 1 *teaspoon ground cumin*
- 1 *tablespoon ground coriander powder*
- ½ *teaspoon cayenne pepper*
- ½ *teaspoon cardamom pods*
- ¼ *teaspoon ground cloves*
- ½ *teaspoon ground cinnamon*
- ¼ *teaspoon ground nutmeg*
- ¼ *teaspoon ground mace*
- 4 *cloves garlic*
- 1 *teaspoon salt*
- ¼ *teaspoon black pepper*
- 3 *tablespoons lemon juice*
- ½ *cup water*

SAUTÉ onions, garlic, and ginger in oil until the onions become slightly brown. Remove this mixture and place in blender. Save the oil in the pan to cook chicken in.

IN A small dry pan roast the almonds until they are brown. Remove to blender. In the same pan add the cumin and coriander and roast on medium heat, shaking pan. This will smoke a little, but don't worry, cook it until the mixture becomes a little darker. Remove to blender. Now add all the remaining spices and garlic to the blender, along with the water, lemon juice, and the saffron water mixture. Blend mixture to a smooth paste.

For the Naan Bread

1½ teaspoons yeast
3 tablespoons water
2 teaspoons sugar
1 egg, beaten
¾ teaspoon salt
1 teaspoon baking powder
2 tablespoons oil
4 tablespoons yogurt
½ cup milk, warmed
3 cups unbleached flour

Preparation

PROOF the yeast in water and sugar. Mix egg, salt, baking powder, oil, and yogurt and add the warm milk. Mix in flour and yeast mixture. Knead well for about 10 minutes. Place in warm place covered for about 2 hours. Preheat broiler. Knead the dough a little and divide into 6 balls. Roll out each ball the shape of a tear drop about 11"X4". Place two breads on a greased cookie sheet. Cover and let rise 15 minutes. Brush each naan with a little water. Place under the broiler about 4 inches from the top. Cook about two minutes on each side or until golden brown. Serve brushed with melted butter

Serves 8

Wine Suggestions: A nice Riesling or Sauvignon Blanc.

Shrikhanda

(Yogurt Pudding)

This dessert is served at the very special occasions in India. Even though it is very simple to make, it is coveted for its smooth creamy texture and sweet tangy taste. Make sure that you pick a good quality yogurt with live cultures and no thickeners or stabilizers. Nancy's yogurt works well, or make your own.

Ingredients

- *2 quarts yogurt*
- *½ teaspoon saffron*
- *¼ teaspoon hot water*
- *½ teaspoon ground nutmeg*
- *1-2 cups sugar*

Preparation

LEAVE yogurt in warm place for a day or two to make sour yogurt.

PUT sour yogurt in a piece of cheese cloth and hang overnight until all water has drained out and it has the consistency of cream cheese. Grind saffron and soak in hot water. Remove yogurt cheese to a bowl and add saffron water, nutmeg, and 1 to 2 cups of sugar to taste. The more sour the yogurt the more sugar you will have to add. That's it! Just spoon or pipe into small custard cups and garnish with sliced almonds.

Serves 4

Pambiche

2811 N.E. Glisan St.
Portland, OR 97232-2433
503-233-0511
www.pambiche.com

Sunday -Thursday
11:00 am -10:00 pm
Friday - Saturday
11:00 am - midnight

Pambiche

Cuban-American chef-owner of Pambiche, John Connell-Maribona, has brought 500 years of creolization to Portland, Oregon. Opened on Saint Valentine's Day 2000, this wildly authentic Cuban café features a full menu of Cuban creole cuisine. The cuisine of Cuba, commonly termed "comida criolla" (Cuban Creole Cuisine), is a result of European influence on New World conditions. With roots in Indigenous Caribbean, Spanish and African cooking, Cuban Creole Cuisine is a seasoned combination of tropical elements. Located in an old storefront on the north end of Portland's East 28th neighborhood, the restaurant is a cozy and warm place that exudes a sense of community – a great place to learn about and enjoy the food and culture of Cuba.

Chef Connell-Maribona brings 20 years of professional culinary experience to Pambiche, having worked as a chef and a pastry chef in some of the area's top restaurants. John also has a Bachelor of Arts degree in Hispanic and Latin American Studies from Portland State University and has traveled extensively throughout the Caribbean and Central America.

In addition to the full Cuban menu at Pambiche chef Connell-Maribona also offers his own dessert line, Postres Apambichaos. Postres Apambichaos are desserts of the highest quality, using only the finest ingredients available. All products are made in house and from scratch incorporating premium liqueurs, exotic fruits and nuts, pure extracts and pastes, fine domestic and imported chocolates, and a variety tropical seasonings. Chef Connell-Maribona brings forward the flavors of Cuba, both in the authentic Tradicional dessert offerings as well as in his original Apambichao creations. Postres Apambichaos display a distinguishing balance between taste, design, and authenticity.

Pambiche is open for lunch and dinner seven days a week. Beginning in the winter of 2004, Pambiche will be offering Cuban breakfast on Saturday and Sunday. Cuban breakfast classics such as pisto manchego, tortilla española, huevos habaneros, fufú criollo and much more will be featured. ¡Buen Provecho!

Caldo Gallego

This is a Cuban-Galician white bean potage made with salt pork, smoked ham, tasajo jerked beef, morcilla & chorizo sausages, and seasoned with fresh collard greens, turnips, potatoes, and green cabbage. Any number of white beans can be used in this recipe. Most Cuban and Spanish recipes simply call for judías, "white beans", or judías buenas, "good white beans". I use great Northern beans. This potage is but one example of a regional Spanish dish that has evolved into a national Cuban staple, as equally Cuban as it is Galician. Serve this potage with fresh bread and your favorite red wine.

Ingredients

1 pound great Northern beans
1 gallon water
2 teaspoons salt
½ teaspoon pepper
4 ounces salt pork
2 ham hocks
1 pound tasajo jerked beef
¼ cup olive oil
1 yellow onion
1 green pepper
2-4 ounces chorizo
2-4 ounces morcilla (blood sausage)
2 large potatoes
4 turnips
1 pound collard greens
1 pound cabbage
½ bunch chopped parsley

Preparation

PICK out any stones or twigs that may be found in beans. Wash the beans thoroughly with cold water, then soak the beans in water overnight. Make sure that the beans are more than completely covered. The beans will absorb water as they expand.

PLACE the beans, water, salt, pepper, salt pork, ham hocks, and tasajo in a heavy soup pot and bring to a boil. Reduce heat to medium and cook covered for 30 minutes.

IN A heavy skillet heat the olive oil until hot and aromatic. Sauté the onion and green pepper in the hot oil until the onion becomes soft and transparent. Deglaze the onion and peppers with some of the bean broth and add to the soup.

ADD the chorizo, morcilla, peeled and cut potatoes, cut turnips, chopped greens, cabbage, and chopped parsley. Simmer for approximately 30 minutes longer, until the vegetables are tender.

Serves 6-8

Patas con Garbanzos

A hearty Cuban-Andalusian chick-pea potage made with pig's feet, bacon, smoked ham, chorizo sausage and seasoned in the Spanish-Creole tradition with saffron, sherry wine, raisins and green olives. A Cuban staple with a true provincial Spanish heritage. This dish is complemented perfectly by any fresh crisp-crusted bread, Cuban or French, and a nice Chilean or Argentinean red wine.

Ingredients

- 1 *pound garbanzos*
- 4 *pounds pigs feet*
- 2 *gallons water*
- *salt to taste*
- ½ *teaspoon black pepper*
- ½ *teaspoon paprika*
- 2 *bay leaves*
- 1 *ham hock*
- ½ *pound bacon*
- 4 *4-ounce dry cured chorizo*
- 1 *cup raisins*
- 1 *cup green olives*
- 4 *cups diced tomatoes*
- 1 *cup tomato sauce*
- ⅔ *cup olive oil*
- 2 *yellow onions*
- 3 *green peppers*
- ⅓ *cup fresh garlic*
- 4 *strands saffron*
- 4 *potatoes*

Preparation

PICK out any stones or twigs that may be found in beans. Wash the beans thoroughly with cold water. Soak the beans in water overnight. Make sure that the beans are more than completely covered. The beans will absorb water as they expand.

PLACE the pig's feet, water, salt, pepper, paprika and bay leaves in a large heavy pot and bring them to a rolling boil. Reduce heat to medium and simmer for 30 minutes. Cool and refrigerate overnight.

DRAIN off soaking water from garbanzo beans, rinse beans, and add to pig's feet. Add ham hock, bacon and chorizo, raisins, olives, tomatoes and tomato sauce. Bring to a boil, reduce heat, and simmer for 30 minutes until garbanzo beans are tender.

HEAT the olive oil in a heavy skillet. When hot and aromatic sauté the onions, green pepper, and garlic until the onion is soft and transparent.

TAKE one cup of hot broth and add the saffron strands, set it aside.

ADD sautéed onion, green pepper and garlic, hot broth with saffron, and the peeled and cut potatoes to the potage. Continue cooking over medium heat for about 15 minutes.

Serves 8

Guiso de Quimbombó

This stew hails from a line of ritual okra dishes brought to Cuba from Africa. Afro-Cuban okra stew is made with adobo marinated pork, fresh lime and ripe plantains. A true gift from the African diáspora! Serve with white rice.

Ingredients

- *8 ounces pork fat*
- *1½ pounds adobo pork*
- *1 yellow onion*
- *1 green pepper*
- *¼ cup fresh garlic*
- *3 ripe plantains*
- *1 cup wine*
- *4 cups water*
- *1 pound okra*
- *4 limes, juiced*
- *2 cups tomato, diced*
- *salt to taste*
- *1 teaspoon pepper*
- *limes for garnish*

Preparation

CHOP pork fat into small pieces. Using the blade attachment of a food processor, grind the fat into a smooth paste. Heat this manteca in a heavy soup pot until it is hot and bubbling.

CUT the adobo marinated pork into one inch pieces. Add them to the hot manteca and cook for 15 minutes.

ADD diced onion, diced green pepper and ground garlic. Simmer 15 more minutes until onions are soft and transparent.

IN A separate pot, boil the plantains until tender. Drain the water and mash the plantains. Roll the mash into little balls slightly smaller than golf balls. Set them aside, keeping them at room temperature.

ADD the wine and reduce slightly. Add water, cut okra, lime juice, diced tomato, salt and pepper. Cook until the okra is tender, 30-45 minutes. Add plantain dumplings just before serving, serve with fresh lime.

Serves 5-6

Potaje de Frijoles Negros

Cuba's famous black beans! Black beans are an absolute staple in Cuban cookery, and to this end Frijoles Negros are the single most important item on Pambiche's menu. Made with black turtle beans, and a typical Spanish sofrito, Frijoles Negros are a healthy, complete protein when served with white rice. I use my grandmother's recipe, which utilizes the pressure cooker, introduced to Cuban kitchens in the late 1940's. So important was the pressure cooker to the modern Cuban woman of the 1950's that my grandmother packed hers in her suitcase when moving to the U.S. in 1955.

Ingredients

- *1 pound black turtle beans*
- *6½ cups water*
- *2-4 sprigs fresh oregano*
- *2 bay leaves*
- *1½ teaspoons sugar*
- *2½ teaspoons salt*
- *1½ tablespoons vinegar*
- *½ teaspoon cumin*
- *½ teaspoon black pepper*
- *¼ cup olive oil*
- *1 yellow onion*
- *1 green pepper*
- *3½ tablespoons fresh garlic*
- *¼ cup sherry wine*
- *3½ cups water*

Preparation

PICK out any stones or twigs that may be found in beans. Wash the beans thoroughly with cold water. Soak the beans in water overnight. Make sure that the beans are more than completely covered. The beans will absorb water as they expand, so be sure to use both a container large enough for this expansion and enough water for the beans to soak up.

PLACE the water in a pressure cooker. Add the beans, minced oregano, bay leaves, sugar, salt, vinegar, cumin and black pepper, cover with the lid and cook over medium high until the cooker begins releasing steam and singing. Set a timer for 1½ hours. At the end of this time place the cooker under cold running water to cool down. When the cooker stops releasing steam, it is safe to open.

HEAT the olive oil in a heavy saucepan until hot and aromatic. Add diced onion, diced green pepper, and minced garlic. Sauté until the onion is soft, transparent, and begins to caramelize slightly.

DEGLAZE with the sherry wine and reduce slightly. When this broth comes to a boil, add 3½ cups water and cook for another 15 minutes.

ADD this sofrito broth to the beans and cook for another hour and a half covered at medium low heat.

IMPORTANT! The beans should come out very soft, some of them will even begin to break down, but most of the beans should still hold their shape. The potage should be thick like a rich soup - not too thick like chile con carne, but not at all watery.

Serves 8-12

Potaje de Frijoles Negros

Guiso de Quimbombó

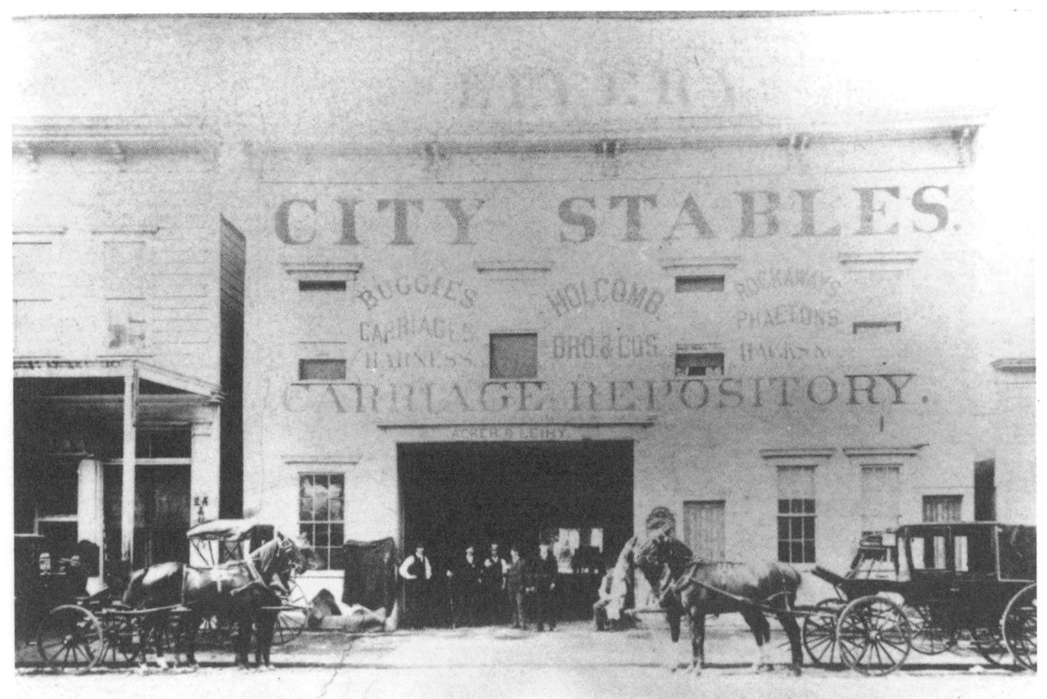

City Stables - 107 Second St. - 1879.

Caprial's Bistro

For the culinary aficionado, this is a must. How often can you combine three things you love: enjoying a fantastic meal, shopping for kitchenware, and learning about the great schedule of cooking classes that you can attend? Caprial and John Pence have created a Mecca for curious home chefs.

Located in the quaint neighborhood of southeast Portland, the Bistro has been open for over a decade. In January 2001, the cooking school and kitchenware shop opened, around the corner from the Bistro. The culinary program offers both demonstrations and hands-on classes taught by Caprial and John, as well as national and local guest chefs and also the resident chef, Lisa Lanxon.

Caprial and John came by their love of cooking from two very different ways. Born in Washington and raised in Portland, Caprial was fascinated with cooking from an early age. Both her maternal grandfather and her parents inspired and encouraged her culinary talents. In 1982, as only one of four women in her class, Caprial was accepted into the Culinary Institute of America in Hyde Park, NY for its rigorous 24-month program. It was here that she met John, a native of Chester, NJ. He had come to the CIA in a more roundabout route. He had no interest in cooking, until he got a part-time job at a local restaurant to help him get through junior college. It was here that he discovered his interest in, and love of, cooking. The two became soul mates over the course of their culinary education. Caprial had no interest in the business side of cooking, but John thrived on it. Shortly after graduation, John headed for Seattle, where he and Caprial were married. Caprial soon was employed at Fullers at the Sheraton Hotel, at the time a cutting-edge restaurant. Her rise there was meteoric, and in 1990, she earned the coveted James Beard Award for Best Chef, Pacific Northwest, the first year the award was granted. After writing the first of many cookbooks, she also began teaching cooking classes at Fullers. International success followed with more cooking demonstrations, travel, and television appearances. John had joined Caprial at Fuller's, but the two realized that someone had to stay home with the young and growing family. In 1991, pregnant with their second child, the two decided to make a life change, and moved back to Portland, where they found the location of their present-day bistro.

Life has not slowed down for the Pence's. John's strong business sense has made a great success of the bistro and the cooking school. This success has spawned several television series on cooking, and multiple books, including the latest: "Caprial & John's Kitchen: Recipes for Cooking Together".

Crab Bruschetta with Fromage Blanc

Ingredients

- 1 *pound fresh crab meat*
- 2 *cloves garlic, minced*
- 2 *tablespoons chopped fresh basil*
- 1 *teaspoon chopped fresh thyme*
- 6 *large shallots, thinly sliced*
- ¼ *cup flour*
- *oil for frying*
- 18 *slices of baguette*
- 2 *tablespoons extra virgin olive oil*
- 1 *whole clove garlic*
- ½ *cup fromage blanc cheese*

Preparation

SQUEEZE the water from the crabmeat and break up into a bowl. Add minced garlic, basil, thyme, and mix well. Refrigerate until ready to use.

TOSS the shallots with the flour and cook in oil that is about 350 degrees. Cook until golden brown, about 2-3 minutes. Drain on paper towels.

HEAT a grill until very hot. Drizzle sliced baguette with olive oil and grill baguette until brown. Rub the toast with garlic while still warm.

TO SERVE, spread toast with the fromage blanc, then top with the crab mixture. Garnish with crispy shallots and serve.

Serves 6

Arugula Tossed with Honey-Rosemary Dressing

Ingredients

- ¾ *pound fresh arugula, washed and spun dry*
- ⅓ *cup shaved Parmesan cheese*
- *Honey Rosemary Dressing (recipe follows)*

Preparation

PREPARE the Honey-Rosemary Dressing. To serve, place the cleaned greens in a bowl and add enough dressing to coat and toss well. Place on the plates and garnish with shaved Parmesan cheese.

For the Honey Rosemary Dressing

- 1 *small shallot, minced*
- 1 *clove garlic, minced*
- 2 *tablespoons honey*
- 3 *tablespoons rice vinegar*
- 2 *teaspoons Dijon mustard*
- 2 *teaspoons chopped fresh rosemary*
- ½ *cup extra virgin olive oil*
- *salt and black pepper to taste*

PLACE shallot, garlic, honey, vinegar, mustard, and rosemary in a bowl and whisk until smooth. While whisking slowly add the olive oil and whisk until smooth. Season with salt and cracked black pepper. Set a side until ready to use.

Serves 6

Rack of Lamb

Encrusted with Pine Nuts and Basil Coulis

Ingredients

- *2 racks of lamb*
- *salt and black pepper*
- *1 tablespoon extra virgin olive oil*
- *2 tablespoons Dijon mustard*
- *2 heads roasted garlic*
- *1 cup toasted pine nuts, ground*
- *Basil Coulis (recipe follows)*

Preparation

PRE-HEAT oven to 400°

TO PREPARE the racks, heat a large sauté pan with olive oil until smoking hot. Season the lamb rack with salt and black pepper. Place in the pan and sear well on both sides about 3 minutes. Remove from the heat and cool slightly. Place the Dijon and roasted garlic in a small bowl and mash to mix together. Smear the Dijon mixture over the seared lamb, then press the toasted pine nuts on top. Place in the pan then in the oven and bake about 15 minutes or until they reach an internal temperature of 130 degrees for medium rare doneness.

WHEN the lamb is finished cooking, let it rest about 3 minutes. Slice and serve warm with the basil coulis.

For the Basil Coulis

- *1 cup basil leaves*
- *2 cloves garlic, chopped*
- *2 tablespoons red wine vinegar*
- *⅓ cup extra virgin olive oil*
- *Pinch red pepper flakes*
- *Salt and black pepper*

WHILE the lamb is cooking prepare the coulis; place all of the ingredients in a blender except the salt and pepper. Blend until smooth. Season with salt and pepper. Set a side until ready to use.

Serves 4

FLOURLESS CHOCOLATE CAKES

with Strawberry Sauce

Ingredients

14 ounces bittersweet chocolate
¼ cup hot water
¼ cup rum
¼ cup heavy cream
6 large eggs
½ cup sugar
Strawberry Sauce (recipe follows)

Preparation

PRE-HEAT oven to 325°

TO PREPARE the cakes, butter 10 (6-ounce) ramekins well. Place the chocolate, water, and rum in a bowl and place over simmering water bath. When just about melted whisk until smooth and remove from the heat. Whisk the cream in a bowl until it holds soft peaks. Set aside until ready to use.

PLACE the eggs and sugar in the bowl of a mixer fitted with a whip and whip until thick and forms a ribbon, about 5 minutes. Gently fold the eggs into the chocolate mixture, then fold in the whipped cream. Carefully spoon into prepared ramekins. Place in a roasting pan filled with very hot water till it reaches about halfway up the sides of the ramekins. Bake for about 45 minutes the center will still be soft, then cool well.

SERVE chocolate cakes with strawberry sauce.

For the Strawberry Sauce

3 cups sliced strawberries
⅓ cup superfine sugar
1 teaspoon vanilla extract
Pinch nutmeg

PLACE the ingredients in a blender and blend until smooth. If the strawberries need a bit of sugar, adjust to taste.

Makes about 10 cakes

Castagna

castagna

café castagna
1752 SE Hawthorne
Portland, OR 97214
503-231-7373

Restaurant hours
Wednesday – Saturday
5:30 pm – 9:30 pm
Café hours
Tuesday – Thursday
5:00 pm – 10:00 pm
Friday and Saturday
5:00 pm – 11:00 pm
Sunday
5:00 pm – 9:30 pm

Castagna

Kevin Gibson and Monique Siu share a common approach to food, and, after working and cooking together for nearly a decade, they co-founded the restaurant Castagna. The restaurant was recognized just months later by The Oregonian, which named it Restaurant of the Year in 2000. Since then, Castagna has been praised in numerous publications, both locally and nationally, including Gourmet, Northwest Palate, Willamette Week, The Oregonian, and Bon Appetit.

Siu and Gibson met in 1990 at Zefiro. Siu was Zefiro's co-founder and pastry chef. Zefiro was Gibson's first job behind the scenes after years of working the front of the house in restaurants across the country. He quickly fell in love with the process and artistry of cooking, and with Siu. The two married in 1995.

Gibson and Siu decided to open Castagna four years later. Her varied background, including experience as an artist and printmaker, years as a chef, pastry chef, wine steward and restaurant owner, gave her the impetus to try something different. Her artistic sensibility is reflected in the restaurant's ambiance, which is simple, elegant, and pure.

Gibson and Siu have an approach that's grounded in French and Italian traditions and techniques, and utilizes the Pacific Northwest's fresh, local ingredients. The restaurant is defined by their desire to express the purity and simplicity of each dish.

The art of balance, simple ingredients blending harmoniously into sophisticated fare, is as important in the décor of the restaurant as it is in the cuisine. The interior expresses a minimalist elegance with creamy walls, dark wood, and sound absorbing cork floors. Artwork by Ming Fay enhances the simple, lovely space, creating the perfect setting in which to enjoy the restaurant's exquisitely prepared dishes.

Castagna is a place where everyone contributes, where the goal is to create a satisfying, engaging experience together, much to the delight and enjoyment of the diners.

Butter Lettuce Salad

with Vinaigrette Royale

This is one of our signature dishes. It is available in both the cafe and the restaurant. It's at its best during the spring and summer when we get our lettuce from the Canby Farm -Your Kitchen Garden.

Ingredients

- *2 heads butter lettuce*
- *1 egg yolk*
- *2 teaspoons smooth Dijon mustard*
- *⅓ cup olive oil*
- *¼ cup peanut oil*
- *4 teaspoons champagne vinegar*
- *water*
- *sea salt and freshly ground black pepper*
- *4 teaspoons chives*
- *4 teaspoons tarragon*
- *fleur de sel (sea salt)*

Preparation

TO MAKE vinaigrette royale, whisk egg yolk with mustard, gradually add oils, whisking to emulsify. Add champagne vinegar and thin with a little water. Season with salt and pepper.

TOSS lettuce with dressing, chives, and tarragon. Sprinkle lightly with fleur de sel.

Serves 4

Cauliflower Soup

This is often on the menu at Castagna. We vary the garnishes: seared scallops, croutons and chives or caviar mixed with whipped crème fraîche.

Ingredients

1 head of pristine cauliflower
1 small onion
1½ tablespoons butter
water to cover
salt

Preparation

BREAK cauliflower into florets and blanch in boiling salted water and drain. Sauté onion gently in butter until soft, but not browned. Add blanched cauliflower.

BARELY cover with water and simmer until cauliflower is easily pierced with a knife. Puree in a blender and put through a sieve. Season to taste

Serves 6–8

Wine suggestion: This is especially good with a dry Riesling

Seared Scallops with Oyster Mushrooms

This recipe is a signature dish. We serve many variations, sometimes with porcini mushrooms, celery or sea beans.

Ingredients

½ pound fresh oyster mushrooms
extra virgin olive oil
6 thyme sprigs
12 large dry pack scallops
1 shallot, minced
1 tablespoon minced chives
1 medium fennel bulb
1 tablespoon lemon juice
1 tablespoon extra virgin olive oil
fleur de sel (sea salt)

Preparation

TOSS half pound of oyster mushrooms in olive oil, thyme, and salt. Place in pan and cover with parchment and seal with foil. Roast at 250 degrees for two hours.

WHEN cool, remove trunk of mushrooms. Remove the foot of the scallops and place on parchment, then place in fridge.

HAVE ready one shallot and chives. Place a slick of olive oil on dinner plate and add scallops, flat side in oil. Do not toss in oil.

HEAT a sauté pan to medium high; place the oiled side of scallops in pan. Turn scallops over when they are loose, and add oyster mushrooms to pan. Cook to desired doneness (medium rare to rare is nice).

WHILE scallops are cooking, slice fennel thinly on bias, toss in bowl with shallot and chives, add lemon juice, extra virgin olive oil and salt. Add mushrooms to fennel salad.

PLACE salad in center of warm plate, arrange 3 scallops around salad, and finish scallops with fleur de sel.

Serves 4

Wine suggestions: Serve with Francois Chidaine, Le Bouche R. Vouvray 2002 Chenin Blanc

Horse drawn streetcars.

2348 SE Ankeny St.
Portland, OR 97214
503-236-4997
http://ilpiatto.citysearch.com

Tuesday – Friday
11:30 am - 2:00 pm
5:30 pm - 9:30 pm

Il Piatto

Eugen Bingham got his first taste of the restaurant business as a 13-year-old boy. His parents owned a ski lodge in the Sierra Nevada Mountains. When he was 15, he and his mother moved to Germany. He studied the German language and began a cook's apprenticeship when he was 17 years old.

For three years he attended cooking school once a week and upon graduation, he went to the Swiss Alps to work at a resort there. He did some traveling, including trips to India, the Himalayas, and South America.

He decided to settle in the United States, selecting San Francisco as his residence of choice, where he worked at many of the finer hotels and restaurants. It was then that he met and married his wife, and they moved to Oregon with their three children in 1991, where he opened Il Piatto in 1994.

Located in southeast Portland, Il Piatto has been described as having "inventive, but not trendy fare... at this charming little neighborhood tratorria" by Zagat Guide. The restaurant has a warm, romantic ambiance in which to enjoy the Italian dishes. Listed in "Portland's Best Places" the comment was, "since its opening in 1994, sweet little Il Piatto has developed an almost cult-like following, in part because of its warm and reassuring atmosphere."

Il Piatto combines the fresh seafood and local vegetables of the area with the traditional tastes of Italy. The extensive wine list complements the menu with regional wines from Italy and other fine selections.

On nearly every forum for review and comments about the restaurant, Il Piatto receives accolades. From attentive, knowledgeable, and friendly service, to the consistently good food and charming ambiance, it seems Il Piatto has become a favorite of those in the know. And success hasn't spoiled it. While busy, Il Piatto still manages to make you feel comfortable, cozy, and glad you came.

Award of Excellence

Saffron Risotto

Ingredients

- 1¾ cups white wine
- 1¾ cups clam juice
- 2 large pinches saffron
- ½ diced yellow onion
- 2 tablespoons chopped garlic
- 2 tablespoons olive oil
- 2 cups Arborio rice
- 1 cup Parmesan cheese
- ¼ cup butter
- salt and pepper to taste

Preparation

BRING white wine, clam juice, and saffron to a boil. Sauté onions, garlic in olive oil, add rice to the onions, coating the rice with the oil. Pour the hot liquid on top of the risotto and stir so that the rice cooks evenly. Cook by medium heat, stirring occasionally.

TO par-cook to finish later, remove after 15 minutes and pour onto a medium sheet pan and place into the refrigerator. To use at the moment, continue cooking for 5 minutes. Stir in Parmesan and butter. Salt and pepper to taste.

ADDITIONAL liquid (water or wine), as much as a ½ cup, will be needed in reheating the par-cooked rice.

Serves 4

Potato Gnocchi

in a Basil Tomato Sauce

Ingredients

- *2 pounds potatoes*
- *2 eggs*
- *¾ cup + ½ cup flour*
- *2 teaspoons salt*
- *1 teaspoon nutmeg*
- *water to cook*
- *⅛ cup oil*
- *Tomato Basil Sauce (recipe follows)*

Preparation

THE night before, parboil the potatoes and refrigerate. Make sure the potatoes are very soft.

THE next day, peel the chilled potatoes and place them in a mixer. Mix them till they are a smooth consistency. Add the eggs, ¾ cup flour, salt, and nutmeg. Place a large pot with salted water on the stove to boiling.

WHEN the dough is smooth, remove and place on a floured surface. Roll into a large log and cut into 2 inch pieces. Use the remainder of the flour to roll out the gnocchi. Roll out each of the dough sections into snake-like shapes ¾ inches in diameter. Cut the dough snakes into ½ inch thick pieces. When they have all been cut, drop them in the boiling water. When the gnocchi rise to the top, let them simmer for 30 seconds, then place them in ice water. As they are chilled, remove them, and let the remaining water drain off. A small amount of oil in the water will prevent them from sticking. Refrigerate. These can be made several days prior.

WHEN ready to serve, reheat and top with tomato basil sauce.

For the Tomato Basil Sauce

- *2 28-ounce cans peeled tomatoes*
- *½ onion, diced*
- *½ cup chopped garlic*
- *2 sprigs chopped rosemary*
- *¼ cup olive oil*
- *2 sprigs julienne basil*
- *salt and pepper to taste*

CRUSH tomatoes by hand until course. Sauté onion, garlic, and rosemary in a medium sized pot in olive oil, add tomatoes and basil and simmer for 3 hours on low to medium heat. Add salt and pepper as needed.

Serves 4

Salmon Cure

Ingredients

- *28 ounces of salmon filet*
- *¼ cup kosher salt*
- *¾ cup brown sugar*
- *2 tablespoons cracked black pepper*
- *Turkish Fig Compote (recipe follows)*

Preparation

COMBINE salt, sugar, and pepper in a bowl. Place part of the mixture in a small tray and lay the filet on top. Cover the filet with the rest of the mixture and refrigerate overnight. Remove the following day and rinse with cold water. The filet can then be cut into four 7-ounce portions, either grilled, sautéed or oven roasted.

TO SERVE, top with Turkish fig compote.

For the Turkish Fig Compote

- *11 ounces of figs*
- *½ red onion, grilled or sautéed in olive oil*
- *1 cup port wine*
- *4 tablespoons black fig vinegar*
- *4 tablespoons olive oil*

BAKE the figs in a covered small roasting pan at 400 degrees, covered with aluminum foil, for 1 hour. Uncover and chill. Grill or sauté red onion, chop fine. Remove the stems from the figs and cut in medium sized dice. Combine all ingredients in a bowl and refrigerate. Serve over salmon.

Serves 4

Champagne Poached Pear with Warm Zabaglione

Ingredients

2 pears
1 bottle of Champagne
Zabaglione (recipe follows)

Preparation

PEEL and cut pears in half to remove the seeds. Poach in champagne for 30 minutes. Serve warm or cold with warm zabaglione over the top.

For the Zabaglione

4 egg yolks
¼ cup sugar
½ cup Marsala

BRING Marsala and sugar to a boil. Place a separate pot on the stove with a small amount of water to use as a water bath. Place egg yolks in a mixing bowl and place in water bath. When Marsala comes to a boil, pour it over the egg yolks. Whisk till frothy and somewhat firm. Keep in a warm location (like above a stove) until ready to be served.

Serves 4

Tira Misu

Ingredients

7 egg whites
½ cup sugar
7 egg yolks
½ cup sugar
1½ cups flour, sifted
1¼ cups fine cornmeal
pinch of salt
Custard (recipe follows)
Syrup (recipe follows)

Preparation

PREHEAT oven to 350 degrees. To make cornmeal cake, whip egg whites and sugar to a soft peak. Cream egg yolks and sugar until frothy. Fold both together with flour, cornmeal, and salt, then spread onto a ½ sheet pan lined with parchment paper. Cook in preheated oven for 15-20 minutes. Make custard and syrup.

TO ASSEMBLE, cut the cornmeal cake in half, and place into the baking pan, soak the cornmeal cake with syrup. Then spread a ¾ inch layer of the custard, and repeat this process over again.

For the Custard

¾ cup sugar
¾ cup Marsala
8 egg yolks
1¼ pounds mascarpone cheese
4 cups whipped cream

HEAT sugar and Marsala in a sauce pan, to simmer, then temper and combine with egg yolks. Whisk over a bain marie till ribbon stage, then cool. Place in mixer with cheese, fold with whipped cream.

For the Syrup

2 cups cold coffee
2 cups simple syrup
¼ cup rum
¼ cup coffee liqueur

COMBINE, then use as directed.

Serves 9

Abe Lincoln statue in the park blocks.

Sala
Sala
3200 SE Milwaukie Ave
Portland, OR 97202
503-235-6665
www.salabistro.citysearch.com
Lunch
Wednesday - Friday
11:30 am - 2:00 pm
Dinner
Wednesday - Sunday
5:30 pm - close

Sala

Eugen Bingham opened Sala after the success of Il Piatto. After his first experiences in the restaurant business as a young man, Eugen knew what he wanted to do the rest of his life. He spent his young adulthood in Europe, traveling and working at various resorts and restaurants.

He finally returned to the United States, landing in San Francisco, where he met and married his wife. In 1991, they moved to Oregon with their three children, and he opened Il Piatto three years later.

Sala opened in 2002, in the Brooklyn neighborhood of Portland, across the street from the Aladdin Theatre. The quaint restaurant has a sage-green dining room, accented with antique chandeliers and colorful artwork.

Sala means ''living room" and the restaurant manages to convey the qualities of being classy and upscale, but not ostentatious or arrogant. The menu includes duck, rabbit, chicken, and fish, but also has meatless entrees that rank equally well in taste and satisfaction. Fresh Northwest produce plays a major role, with morel, portabella, and chanterelle mushrooms taking center stage, joined by salmon and shrimp, but always in balanced creations that allow the natural flavors of the ingredients to shine.

An extensive wine list has choices to please everyone, with many selections from Italy and France. The cocktail list even offers more than the stand-bys, with the pomegranate sangria a surprising and delightful option. During the warm summer months, enjoy the food and libations in the garden courtyard, which has a fountain, vines, wisteria and abundant flowers.

On Sundays, Sala has an affordable prix fix, with soup/salad, pasta or meat entrée and ice cream dessert. Great for the kids, but the adults don't have to sacrifice, either.

Award of Excellence

Goat Cheese Fritelle

Ingredients

- 2 *cups goat cheese*
- ¼ *cup diced red onion*
- 2 *tablespoons vegetable oil*
- 1 *tablespoon chopped garlic*
- ¼ *cup chopped thyme*
- ½ *cup chopped dates*
- ¼ *cup caramelized red onion*
- 1 *tablespoon salt and pepper*
- ½ *cup bread crumbs*
- ½ *cup chopped walnuts*

Preparation

SAUTÉ the onions in a small pan with oil, garlic. Towards the end add the chopped thyme. Place the goat cheese in a mixer and add dates, salt and pepper, and caramelized onions. Combine bread crumbs and chopped walnuts. Create small patties and toss them in bread mixture, cook them in butter and oil.

Serves 6–8

Soft Polenta

Ingredients

- ½ *cup diced onion*
- ¼ *cup chopped garlic*
- ¼ *cup olive oil*
- 2 *sprigs rosemary*
- 4 *cups cream*
- 2 *cups water*
- 1 *tablespoon salt and pepper*
- 2 *cups stewed Roma tomatoes*
- 2 *cups coarse polenta*

Preparation

SAUTÉ onion and garlic in olive oil, add rosemary. Add cream and water, then salt and pepper. When cream comes to a boil, add Roma tomatoes.

AS THE liquid simmers, stir in polenta, lower the temperature and cover. Cook for 30 minutes at a low temperature.

Serves 6–8

Veal Milanese

Ingredients

- 16 ounce veal top round
- ½ cup flour
- 1 cup ground Parmesan
- 5 eggs
- flour for dredging
- ½ butter, ½ vegetable oil combination, to cook
- White Wine Caper Sauce (recipe follows)

Preparation

THINLY slice veal and pound thin with a mallet. Dredge each piece of meat in the flour. Make a batter with the ½ cup flour, Parmesan and eggs, and dip the floured veal pieces in the batter. Cook in a preheated pan, medium temperature, in butter/vegetable oil combination until the Parmesan coating is golden brown. Serve with white wine caper sauce.

For the White Wine Caper Sauce

- 3 cups chicken stock
- 2 cups white wine
- butter to taste
- ¼ cup capers
- ¼ cup lemon juice
- ¼ cup chopped parsley

REDUCE chicken stock and white wine down by half. Whisk in desired amount of butter. Finish with capers, lemon juice, and parsley.

Serves 4

Creamy Lemon Ice Cream

Ingredients

- 2 *cups sugar*
- ½ *cup water*
- 1 *tablespoon minced lemon zest*
- 1 *cup lemon juice*
- 3 *cups heavy cream*
- 1 *cup milk*
- 8 *egg yolks*

Preparation

BRING 1 cup sugar and water to boil with juice and lemon zest. When sugar is dissolved, cool to room temperature and set aside.

HEAT cream with milk and the remaining cup of sugar. Place egg yolks into a mixing bowl. Pour the simmering cream mixture on top of the egg yolks and whisk till smooth. Return the mixture back on the stove, stir constantly with a wooden spoon for about 2 minutes. Transfer mixture into a medium sized stainless steel bowl and place onto an ice water bath till cool.

WHEN the mixture is cooled stir in the lemon syrup and process in an ice cream maker.

Serves 6–8

Cinnamon Biscotti

Ingredients

- 1 *cup granulated sugar*
- 1 *cup dark brown sugar*
- ⅓ *cup vegetable oil*
- 3 *teaspoons ground cinnamon*
- 1 *teaspoon ground cloves*
- 2 *teaspoons water*
- 4 *whole eggs*
- 2 *teaspoons baking powder*
- 2½ *cups flour*
- ½ *cup sliced almonds*

Preparation

PREHEAT oven to 300 degrees. Combine sugar, vegetable oil, cinnamon, cloves, water, eggs, and baking powder into a mixing bowl. Gradually add flour, and when the dough is smooth, add the almonds.

ROLL out dough on a floured surface into portions 12 inches long and ¾ inch in diameter. Place onto a parchment paper lined baking sheet, and bake in oven at 300 degrees for 30 minutes. Remove from oven and set to cool for 10 minutes. Cut each biscotti into ¾ inch slices.

Makes 2 dozen

Salvador Molly's

1523 SW Sunset Blvd.
Hillsdale, OR 97239
503-293-1790
www.salvadormollys.com

Sunday – Thursday
11:30 am – 9:00 pm
Friday and Saturday
11:30 am – 10:00 pm

Salvador Molly's

If you are looking for outrageous fun, fiery Pirate food, and a wild and crazy time, look no further than Salvador Molly's.

Named for the love of a Caribbean princess (Molly) and her spice-stealing Pirate (Salvador), you'd expect Salvador Molly's to be "A World Away from the Everyday", and you wouldn't be disappointed. Since the restaurant opened in Hillsdale in 1996, owner Rick Sadle has opened a second restaurant, catering kitchen and event site, has booths at the local Farmer's Markets, and operates both the Café at the Portland Art Museum and the Lake House at Blue Lake Park.

The cooking blends Caribbean, Latin & African influences. Some of the best-known dishes are the variety of jerk-seasoned items. Jerk, which originates from Jamaica, uses an abundance of spices and smoke to flavor meats, fish, and tofu in a unique way. The Tamarindo Jerk Wings, served with a creamy garlic dip, are not to be missed. The Beer-Battered Rasta Rings are excellent, and there is an extensive menu of Caribbean and Latino dishes.

Row after row of spicy sauces and mixes line one wall of Salvador Molly's, in varying levels of heat. From Habanero Pepper Sauce to Sweet Papaya Mustard, the choices escalate from one to twenty in intensity. If you feel brave, or just foolhardy, try for the honor of having your photo on the Wall of Flames. To qualify, you have to eat a serving of five habanero-cheese fritters, called Great Balls of Fire, with a sauce called Sunshine and Pain. If you survive, you are rewarded with your photo posted on the wall and a chance to compete for the title of King or Queen of Flames. Of course, you can always put out the fire with a beverage from the large selection of beers and tropical cocktails.

Salvador Molly's offers family fun with world music, surf videos, shelled peanuts on the floor and friendly service.

Tahu

Indonesian Fried Tofu Appetizers

Ingredients

- 1 *pound firm tofu, drained, cut into 1" cubes, rinsed and patted dry*
- 1 *teaspoon ground cumin*
- 1 *teaspoon ground coriander*
- 1 *teaspoon ground cardamom*
- 1 *teaspoon ground cayenne pepper*
- 1 *teaspoon ground ginger*
- 1 *teaspoon granulated garlic*
- 1 *teaspoon kosher salt*
- 1 *cup water*

Preparation

TOAST the spices in a hot pan. Combine the spices and salt with the water. Pour the marinade over the tofu and let marinate overnight.

TO PREPARE, heat an inch of vegetable oil in a heavy skillet over medium-high heat. Drain cubes of tofu for a moment, then gently drop into hot oil. Fry until crisp outside and heated through on the inside, about 2 minutes. Place on serving dish and garnish with chopped peanuts. Served with spicy peanut sauce traditionally, but also good with most chutneys and raitas.

Serves 3-6

Wine suggestion: a Southeastern Australian Shiraz

African Groundnut Soup

Ingredients

- 1 pound yellow onions, diced
- ½ pound carrots, diced
- ¼ pound celery, diced
- 3 tablespoons kosher salt
- 2 tablespoons olive oil
- 4 tablespoons minced fresh garlic
- 3 bay leaves
- 2 teaspoons ground cumin
- 1-3 tablespoons crushed red chile flakes
- 2 15-ounce cans coconut milk plus 2 cans water
- 4 cups creamy peanut butter, all-natural preferred

Preparation

IN A large stockpot with a heavy bottom, sweat the onions, carrots, and celery in the olive oil with the salt until soft – do not brown.

ADD garlic, bay leaves, cumin, and red chile flakes; cook another 10 minutes on medium heat.

ADD the coconut milk and water and simmer for 30 minutes.

REMOVE from heat, whisk in peanut butter.

SERVE in a wide soup bowl with scallions, toasted peanuts, and a swirl of sambal (Asian red chile sauce). This soup will keep for 10 days if properly cooled and stored tightly covered and refrigerated.

Serves 12

Beverage suggestion: Enjoy with a light lager such as Red Stripe or Corona.

Poke Banana Salad

Ingredients

- 5 *large bananas, peeled and cubed*
- 1 *pint cider vinegar*
- 1 *cup white granulated sugar*
- 5 *scallions, sliced thinly*
- ½ *red onion, diced small*
- 1 *tablespoon sambal (Asian red chile sauce)*
- 2 *teaspoons nam pla (Vietnamese fish sauce)*
- ¼ *cup honey*
- 1 *teaspoon white sesame seeds*
- 1 *teaspoon black sesame seeds*

Preparation

MIX vinegar and sugar in a large bowl; add diced bananas and mix well, but gently.

SOAK bananas in vinegar mixture while you prepare the remaining ingredients.

MIX together scallions, red onion, sambal, nam pla, honey, and sesame seeds in a large bowl. Drain bananas, reserving 1 cup of the liquid. Mix bananas in gently with the remaining ingredients. Add reserved vinegar, stir, and store, tightly covered, in the refrigerator. Will keep for 1 day. Serve with grilled poultry or fish.

Serves 12

Beverage suggestion: A light Asian beer such as Tsing-Tao.

Poke Banana Salad

Chimichurri Sauce

Ingredients

- *1 bunch parsley*
- *2 bunches cilantro*
- *1 bunch scallions*
- *12 peeled garlic cloves*
- *½ tablespoon ground cumin*
- *1 pint olive oil (not extra virgin)*
- *1 cup fresh lime juice*
- *½ cup fresh orange juice*
- *2 jalapenos, stems and seeds removed*
- *1 tablespoon black pepper*
- *3 tablespoons kosher salt*

Preparation

WASH the parsley, cilantro, and scallions well, dry them and chop roughly. Put all ingredients into a large container and blend into a smooth sauce. Recipe makes about 1 quart – may be halved or doubled. Keeps well for about 1 week, refrigerated; may also be frozen.

THIS sauce is great with steak. To prepare, place raw steaks in a plastic bag, using ⅛ cup marinade per steak. Marinate steaks, refrigerated, for up to 4 hours. Do not marinate overnight or steaks will become soft.

PREHEAT grill, grill pan, or broiler. Remove steaks from marinade. Cook steaks to desired doneness. Allow meat to rest 3-5 minutes on a plate. Slice against the grain and serve with extra chimichurri sauce.

Beverage suggestion: Chimichurri Steak goes well with a Caipirinha, a Brazilian drink popular in Europe and the US.

Arepas

Ingredients

- ½ bag P.A.N. white corn flour (masa par arepa – in all Latin food markets)
- ½ pound shredded part-skim mozzarella cheese
- ¼ cup green onions, minced
- 1 tablespoon brown sugar
- 1 tablespoon cumin
- 1 tablespoon kosher salt
- 1½ tablespoons granulated garlic
- ½ tablespoon black pepper
- ½ tablespoon oregano
- ¼ cup minced green bell peppers
- ¼ cup minced fresh cilantro
- ½ cup vegetable oil
- 3 cups warm water
- 1½ tablespoons paprika

Preparation

BLEND all ingredients until smooth. Form 2 ounce flat, round patties and layer into pans with paper. To serve, cook on a well oiled griddle until brown on both sides.

Makes 24 Arepas

Beverage suggestion: a classic Margarita – with fresh lime and good tequila!

Cotija Calamari Steaks

Ingredients

4 5-ounce calamari steaks
finely ground cotija cheese
beaten eggs
panko (Japanese bread crumbs)

Preparation

THAW calamari steaks and drain any water off. Pound out very thinly between sheets of plastic wrap with the textured side of the meat mallet.

PIE pans work well for the three dipping ingredients. Put finely ground cotija cheese in one pie pan, beaten eggs with no water added in another, and bread crumbs in the third.

DIP calamari steaks carefully in each pan, first the cheese, then the egg, then the bread crumbs.

BE sure to place sheets of parchment or wax paper in between each calamari steak, using some extra bread crumbs to absorb any excess moisture.

FRY steaks in a hot cast-iron skillet or on a well-oiled griddle for 2 minutes per side – be careful not to overcook. Goes well served over black beans with a light vegetable-based salsa or salad.

Serves 4

Beverage suggestion: enjoy with a Mojito.

Tucci
Tucci
220 A Avenue
Lake Oswego, OR 97304
503-697-3383
www.tucci.biz
Monday
11:00 am – 2:00 pm
Tuesday – Thursday
11:00 am – 10:00 pm
Friday and Saturday
11:00 am -11:00 pm
Sunday
4:00 pm - 9:00 pm

Tucci

One of the first things you notice in Tucci is the neon "Lido" sign next to the bar. For a moment you might wonder if you are in the right restaurant.

Don't worry, you are. The story behind the sign has to do with the fact that Grandma Tucci was an employee of the now-defunct Lido restaurant for over 50 years and was as well known as the restaurant itself. Tucci, this unique little Italian dining house, evolved from the belief that food and family are inseparable. Sunday dinners and holidays were times to gather everyone around the big dining room table at the Italian grandparents' home, and everyone was expected to be there.

David and Suzanne Regan, Tucci's owners, wanted to preserve the tradition by creating an atmosphere that celebrated food, family, and friends. The goal of Tucci is to make everyone feel like an honored houseguest.

David and Suzanne are connoisseurs of fine food and wine, and working owners who spend many hours making sure Tucci lives up to the goal they've set. As Tucci is a family-owned restaurant, don't be surprised to see some, or all, of the extended family in aprons!

The menu offers fresh foods from the Pacific Northwest prepared in their open kitchen by executive chef Pascal Chureau. Chureau was born and raised in Bordeaux, in the southwest of France, where he attended the Ecole Hoteliere de Bordeaux, graduating in 1985, and studied French, Italian, and Mediterranean cuisine. In 1999, Chef Chureau moved to Portland with his wife, who attended law school, and became the executive chef at Tucci Restaurant. His philosophy is to use as many local and organic ingredients as possible, along with natural beef and wild fish.

Complementing these dishes is an all-Italian wine selection featuring limited-production artisanal wines, and a full service lounge serving select spirits, liqueurs, and creative infusions.

With the elegant but casual surroundings, you can dine inside or outside on the heated patio.

Tucci offers monthly cooking classes and reserves every Monday evening for special, private parties. Tucci also offers catering in your home. Dinner reservations are recommended.

Forest Mushroom Bruschetta

This is a signature dish and has been on the menu from the beginning.

Ingredients

1 loaf Ciabatta bread
3 shallots, large
3 cups oyster mushrooms
2 cups shitake mushrooms
1 cup chanterelle mushrooms
2 cups Gorgonzola cheese
4 cups arugula
2 cups virgin olive oil
3 tablespoons butter
1 tablespoon truffle oil
salt and pepper to taste

Preparation

IN A sauté pan cook the mushrooms with the shallots, oil salt, pepper. Cut the bread lengthwise and place on the grill. Spread the Gorgonzola cheese on the grilled bread, then add the arugula and the warm mushrooms. To finish, drizzle with the truffle oil

Serves 4

Wine suggestion: Spumante (Italian sparkling wine) or Champagne

Butter Lettuce and Goat Cheese Dressing

This is a favorite on the summer menu at Tucci's.

Ingredients

1 head butter lettuce
⅓ cup dried cherries
1 each Bosc pear
2 ounces hard goat cheese
Goat Cheese Dressing (recipe follows)

Preparation

MAKE the dressing, and add it to the butter lettuce, mix well.

TO SERVE, place the dressed salad in the center of the plate, put the sun-dried cherries around the salad. Shave both the pear and the goat cheese on top, using a chocolate or truffle peeler.

For the Goat Cheese Dressing

¼ cup Champagne vinegar
2 tablespoons Dijon mustard
4 tablespoons soft goat cheese
1½ cup extra virgin olive oil
salt and pepper to taste

IN A blender, combine the vinegar, mustard, and goat cheese. When mixture becomes thick, add the oil slowly. You can keep this, refrigerated, up to a week.

Serves 4

Wine suggestion: Tenimenti Ruffino Chardonnay will balance the strong goat cheese flavor well.

Venison Shanks Ossobuco

This is a highly requested dish. It is served during the colder months, and featured on the fall and winter menu. Lamb can be substituted for the venison.

Ingredients

- 4 *venison shanks*
- ¼ *cup olive oil*
- 2 *carrots, diced*
- 1 *yellow onion, diced*
- ½ *bunch celery, diced*
- ¼ *cup chopped garlic*
- 2 *tablespoons chopped rosemary*
- 2 *tablespoons chopped thyme*
- 2 *tablespoons chopped oregano*
- 1 *cup Nicoise olives*
- 4 *cups diced pancetta or bacon*
- 1 *cup dry white wine*
- 4 *cups veal stock, or chicken stock*
- 3 *cups tomato sauce*
- 5 *cups water*
- ½ *teaspoon black pepper*
- 1 *teaspoon salt*
- *mashed potatoes or polenta*

Preparation

IN A roasting pan sauté the venison shanks in the olive oil. When brown in color, remove from the cooking pan. Add the diced vegetables, herbs, olives, and pancetta to pan, and cook for about 10 minutes, or until vegetables are tender.

ADD the wine, stock, tomato sauce, and, finally, the water. The liquid should cover all the shanks.

COVER with foil, and cook for 4 hours at 380 degrees.

WHEN done, remove the shanks from the sauce, and reduce the sauce by a third. Season with salt and pepper to taste. To serve, place the shanks on mashed potatoes or polenta and cover with sauce.

Serves 4

Wine suggestion: Chianti or a Barolo wine from Italy

James Beard Award

James Beard, often called the father of American gastronomy, died in 1985, but his legacy lives on in the James Beard Foundation.

When he was alive, James Beard was considered the primary and definitive resource for all things having to do with food and cooking. The James Beard Foundation continues as both a source of information and education about gastronomic issues. The foundation offers scholarships, workshops, and recognition for all aspects of food, culinary arts, and wine.

Every year the James Beard Foundation Awards are announced at a huge party that celebrates the industry and James Beard's birthday, called the Beard Birthday Fortnight. The awards recognize culinary professionals for excellence and achievement in their field. More than 60 awards are given to chefs, restaurateurs, cookbook authors, journalists, broadcasters, and restaurant designers. The nominees and winners are chosen by more than 500 food and beverage professionals who cast their vote by secret ballot.

There are six separate recognition programs: The James Beard Foundation Chef And Restaurant Awards, The James Beard Foundation Kitchenaid® Book Awards, The James Beard Foundation Journalism Awards, The James Beard Foundation Viking Range Awards For Broadcast Media, The James Beard Foundation & Rums Of Puerto Rico Restaurant Design Awards, The James Beard Foundation/D'artagnan Who's Who Of Food And Beverage In America And The James Beard Foundation Lifetime Achievement Award.

A chef who wins in one category is not eligible for that same award for five years, but is eligible for other category awards.

For more information on the James Beard Foundation, the programs, awards and history go to the website, www.jamesbeard.org.

Culinary Sources

DISCLAIMER

Resources are listed for your convenience. We do not endorse or recommend any particular listing or company.

FARM-FRESH PRODUCTS

Apeasay Orchards
Organic Orchards, Pears
789 Highline Dr.
Hood River, OR 97031
Phone: 866-221-7158

Gathering Together Farm
25159 Grange Hall Rd
Philomath, OR 97370
Phone: 541-929-4068
Fax: 541-929-4289
www.gatheringtogetherfarm.com

Smith's asparagus
Email: outbackfarms@gorge.net

ETHNIC OR EXOTIC ITEMS

Buy Gourmet Foods
Cheese, pate, fruits and more.
www.buygourmetfoods.com

Cafe Cubano
tasajo, morcilla, chorizo sausages, online shop for Cuban and Latin American products
11200 SW 107 CT.
Miami, Florida 33176
Phone: 305-251-4032
www.cafecubano.com

Cyber Cucina
Carnaroli rice, gourmet Italian and other Mediterranean products
www.cybercucina.com

Cuban Food Market
3100 SW 8 Street
Miami Fl 33135
Phone: 877-999-9945
Phone: 305-644-8870
Fax: 305-644-8861
www.cubanfoodmarket.com

Essential Living Foods, Inc.
Lucuma fruit, aji peppers, exotic ingredients.
PO Box 491
San Luis Obispo, CA 93406
Phone: 805-528-4176
www.essentiallivingfoods.com

Ethnic Grocer
Authentic foods from all over the world.
695 Lunt Avenue
Elk Grove Village, IL 60007
Phone: 312-373-1777
Fax: 312-373-1777
www.ethnicgrocer.com

Fennel pollen
Po Box 608
Goshen, CA 93227
Phone: 1-800-821-5989
www.fennelpollen.com

Grand Gourmet Food
Smoked Fish, Cheeses, Caviar, Chocolates, Exotic Meats, Soups and more.
www.grandgourmetfood.com

igourmet
Manchego cheese, ricotta salata, specialty cheeses, fine foods, exquisite gifts.
1735 Front St.
Yorktown Heights, NY 10598
Phone: 877-igourmet (446-8763)
www.igourmet.com

La Tienda
Marcona almonds, jamon serrano ham, etc.
3701 Rochambeau Road
Williamsburg VA 23188
Phone: 888-472-1022
Phone: 757-566-9606
Fax: 757-566-9603
www.tienda.com

Napa Style
Tellicherry peppercorns
Peppercorns from India's Malabar Coast
801 Main Street
St. Helena, CA 94574
Phone: 866-776-6272
www.napastyle.com

Penzeys Spices
Spices, herbs and seasonings.
Phone: 800-741-7787
Fax: 262-785-7678
www.penzeys.com

San Marzano Imports
San Marzano tomatoes
Nick Soccodato
116 West 4th Street
Howell, NJ 07731
Phone: 732-364-1724
www.sanmarzanoimports.com

Spanish Table
Products from Spain and Portugal
1427 Western Ave
Seattle, WA 98101
Phone: 206-682-2827
seattle@spanishtable.com
www.spanishtable.com

Sweet Freedom Farm
New Mexico chili connection
Albuquerque, New Mexico
www.sweetfreedomfarm.com

The Great American Spice Co.
aji Amarillo chili
"The world's largest spice store"
P.O. Box 80068
Fort Wayne, IN 46898
Phone: 260-420-8118
Phone: 888-502-8058
http://www.americanspice.com/

Wasabi tobiko
www.finest-caviar.com/flying-fish-roe-tobiko.htm

MEAT AND WILD GAME

Broken Arrow Ranch
Venison and wild game
P.O. Box 530
Ingram, TX 78025
Phone: 800-962-4263
www.brokenarrowranch.com

Maple Leaf Farms
Duck
Phone: 800-382-5546
www.mapleleaffarms.com

Syracuse's Sausage
Linguisa sausage, Wisconsin-style bratwurst, chorizo, Andouille and other sausages.
903 N. Hwy 156
P.O. Box 118
Ponder, Texas 76259
Phone: 940-479-2700
Phone: 800-525-8540
www.syracusesausage.com

WINE AND SPIRITS

Ficklin port
Ficklin Vineyards
30246 Avenue 7½
Madera, CA 93637
Phone: 559-674-4598

Calymyrna figs, nuts, dried fruits, herbs and spices, specialty items.
Galloway's Naturally
9851 Van Horne Way
Richmond, BC, Canada
Phone: 604-270-6363
Fax: 604-270-0452

Clear Creek Distillery
Williams Pear Brandy, American Calvados Apple Brandy and other fine fruit brandies
1430 Northwest 23rd
Portland, OR. 97210
Phone: 503-248-9470
Fax: 503-248-0490
www.clearcreekdistillery.com

KITCHEN SUPPLIES AND EQUIPMENT

Kitchen Collection
Silicone baking mats, cookware, bake ware, small appliances, decorative wood, marble, and ceramics, great gadgets.
71 East Water Street
Chillicothe, OH 45601
Phone: 1-888-548-2651
Phone: 740-774-0561
www.kitchencollection.com

Kitchen Emporium
Blini pan
32A Friendship Street
Westerly, Rhode Island 02891
Phone: 888-858-7920
Fax: 401-596-4872
www.kitchenemporium.com

Made In Oregon
PO Box 3458
Portland, OR 97208
Phone: 503-273-8719
Phone: 800-828-9673
Fax: 503-222-6855
www.madeinoregon.com

In Good Taste
231 NW 11th Ave
Portland, OR 97209
Phone: 503-248-2015
www.ingoodtastestore.com

Glossary

adobo pork	Adobo is a Philippine seasoning made of chilies, herbs, and vinegar.
agar agar	A setting agent, similar to gelatin, used widely in Asia. Agar agar is made from dried seaweed and comes in blocks, powder or strands.
aji amarillo peppers	These yellow peppers have a hot fruity flavor. Good in Southwest, Mexican and South American dishes. Aji is the general term for a Peruvian chile, and amarillo means yellow.
al dente	Italian for "to the tooth," describing pasta or other food cooked only until it offers a slight resistance when bitten into, but which is not soft or overdone.
arepas	Arepas are made from maize and used like bread in Venezuelan families. They are usually stuffed with a variety of savory fillings.
bain-marie	A term indicating a container placed inside another container of water so the food cooks gently.
blanch	Plunging food (usually vegetables and fruits) into boiling water briefly, then into cold water to stop the cooking process.
braise	Browning food (usually meat or vegetables) first in fat, then cooking in a small amount of liquid, covered, at low heat for a long time.
brunoise	A mixture of vegetables that have been finely diced or shredded, then cooked slowly in butter.
Calvados	A dry apple brandy from Calvados, the Normandy region of northern France, often used in dishes with chicken, pork and veal.
capers	The flower bud of a bush native to the Mediterranean and parts of Asia, picked, sun-dried, and then pickled.
Carnaroli rice	Carnaroli is a firm grain rice, popular in risotto.
carpaccio	Usually served as an appetizer, this Italian creation has thin shavings of raw beef fillet, drizzled with olive oil and lemon juice or served with a mayonnaise or mustard sauce, and garnished with capers or onions.
chèvre cheese	French for "goat," chèvre is a pure white goat's-milk cheese with a tart flavor.
chiffonade	Similar to julienne, the process of cutting lettuce, endive, or herbs into thin, even strips.
chinois	A very fine mesh cone-shaped metal sieve used for pureeing or straining. Often a spoon or pestle is used to press the food through it.
chipotle	A dried, smoked, jalapeno with a sweet, almost chocolaty flavor.
chorizo	A coarsely ground pork sausage, highly seasoned, used in Mexican and Spanish dishes
clarified	The process of clearing a cloudy substance, such as in stocks or wines, or melting butter until the foam rises and is skimmed off.
cocottes	A French word meaning "casserole", a shallow individual baking dish usually with handles and a lid

confectioners' sugar	Powdered sugar.
confit	A French word from a term meaning "to prepare," used for meat that has been cooked and preserved in its own fat.
concassé	A coarsely chopped mixture, often made up of tomatoes.
conserve	A thick mixture of fruits, nuts and sugar, cooked together and often used on biscuits, or as garnish.
coulis	A general term meaning a thick puree or sauce.
crème anglaise	A custard sauce with cream, sugar, egg yolks, and, usually, vanilla for flavoring.
crème fraîche	A thick, velvety cream that can be boiled without curdling.
crépinette	A small, slightly flattened sausage is made of minced pork, lamb, veal or chicken, sometimes with truffles. Crépinettes are usually cooked by coating them in melted butter and breadcrumbs before sautéing, grilling, or broiling.
crostini	Small, thin slices of toasted bread, usually brushed with olive oil.
curry powder	Popular in Indian cooking, curry powder is a mixture of as many as 20 spices, herbs, and seeds. It comes in two basic styles — standard, and the hotter of the two, "Madras."
de-bearding	To pull the threads towards the hinge of the mussel and tear out.
demi-glace	A rich brown sauce (usually meat stock) combined with Madeira or sherry and slowly cooked until it's reduced by half to a thick glaze.
deglaze	Adding wine or water to the skillet to loosen browned bits on the bottom to make a sauce.
demi-sec	In cooking, it refers to reducing by half. In wine, it refers to the level of sweetness.
etouffee	In Cajun cooking, etouffee means "smothered in a sauce."
foie gras	The term generally used for goose liver.
focaccia	Italian bread with a large, flat round shape, brushed or drizzled with olive oil and sprinkled with salt.
french, to	To trim fat or bone from a cut of meat.
Garam Masala	Garam Masala is a spice blend, used in South Asia. Only a small amount is required, as it is a very strong spice.
gremolata	This garnish is made of minced parsley, citrus zest, garlic, oil, and salt, and it's often sprinkled over osso buco for a fresh accent.
hotel pan	Rectangular stainless steel pans used to cook, store and serve food, and designed to fit in steam tables, racks, and chafers. Usually 12x20 inches with sides generally 2 inches tall, but sometimes 4 or 6 inches tall.
julienne	A method of cutting vegetables into thin strips, usually about 1 inch by 1/16 inch.
kosher salt	An additive-free coarse-grained salt.

lucuma	Lucuma fruit originates from the South American Andean regions of Peru. The green fruit is round or oval, with a bright yellow pulp.
Madeira	Madeira is a distinctive fortified wine and is an excellent cooking wine.
Madras curry	see curry
manteca	Spanish for lard or shortening.
mesclun	A mix of young, small salad greens, such as arugula, dandelion and radicchio.
mirepoix; mirepois	A mixture of diced carrots, onions, celery, and herbs sautéed in butter.
mirin	A sweet, rice wine used in cooking to sweeten meat or fish dishes.
mise en place	To have all the ingredients necessary for a dish and be ready to combine for cooking.
Manchego cheese	Cheese from the La Mancha region of Spain, made from raw sheep's milk. The flavor is zesty and the texture is firm and tends to be dry.
mole	Mole is a smooth, cooked blend of onion, garlic, chilies, ground pumpkin, or sesame seeds, and a small amount of Mexican chocolate, its best-known ingredient.
morcilla	Morcilla is a blood sausage that is often used in stews, or sliced and fried as an accompaniment to eggs or as an appetizer.
morel mushroom	An edible wild mushroom belonging to the same fungus species as the truffle.
napoleon	A dish made with a variety of layers, usually a dessert.
nappe	Usually referring to a coating, such as a sauce thick enough to coat a spoon.
osso buco	Veal shanks cooked slowly in olive oil, white wine, stock, onions, tomatoes, garlic, anchovies, carrots, celery and lemon peel.
paella	A Spanish rice dish with meats, shellfish, or vegetables, usually flavored with saffron
palm sugar	Used primarily for making sweets and desserts, palm sugar's creamy, caramel-like sweetness can be used in curries and sauces. Palm sugar is tapped from palmyra or lontar palm trees, commonly known as sugar palm, and is available in Asian markets.
pancetta	Slightly salty Italian bacon cured with salt and spices, but not smoked.
panko	Coarse Japanese bread crumbs used for coating fried foods.
panna cotta	Literally means "cooked cream" in Italian. A light, silky egg custard, often flavored with caramel, served cold, usually with fruit or chocolate sauce.
pappardelle	A wide noodle, about 5/8 inch, usually with rippled sides.
par-boil	To partially cook food by boiling it in water for a brief time. The food is then held to be finished later, usually with other ingredients.
pave	A French word for square or rectangle, often a paving stone.

Pecorino Romano	Italian cheese made from sheep's milk. Pecorino Romano is a hard, dry cheese with a sharp, pungent flavor.
plantain	The plantain, a very large, firm variety of banana, is sometimes called a "cooking banana" and is popular in Latin American dishes.
prosciutto	Italian word for ham; seasoned, salt-cured and air-dried, but not smoked.
phyllo	Thin layers of pastry dough used in sweet and savory recipes.
purée	To grind or mash food until it's completely smooth, using a food processor, a blender, or by forcing the food through a sieve.
ramekin	An individual earthenware-baking dish similar to a miniature soufflé dish.
reduce (reduction)	To boil a liquid rapidly, reducing it until its thickened and flavorful.
rice paper	An edible, translucent paper made from water combined with the rice-paper plant, an Asian shrub, and used to wrap foods. Rice paper can be found in Asian markets and some supermarkets.
roux	A mixture of equal parts flour and butter used to thicken sauces. Cooking different lengths of time results in different flavors and colors.
sauté	To quickly cook food over direct heat in a small amount of hot oil.
sauterne	A full-bodied sweet white wine from the Bordeaux region of France.
Sambal Oelek	Chilies with no additives such as garlic or spices, it can be used to add heat to a dish without altering the other delicate flavors. Available in Asian markets.
sec	This French word means "dry".
semifreddo	An Italian word, meaning "half cold," this refers to a chilled or partially frozen dessert.
shallot	Member of the onion family.
sofrito	Traditional Spanish sofrito is a sauce made by sautéing annatto seeds in rendered pork fat. The seeds are removed, then onions, green peppers, garlic, pork, and herbs are cooked in the oil until they are tender and the mixture thickens.
sweat	To cook vegetables slowly in a tightly covered pan so that they literally stew in their own juice.
Tabasco pepper; Tabasco Sauce	A small, hot, red pepper originally from the Mexican state of Tabasco. The word, meaning "damp earth," is trademarked by the McIlhenny family.
tamarind	The tamarind is the fruit of a tall shade tree found in Asia, northern Africa, and India. The long pods have a sour-sweet pulp that is popular as a flavoring in East Indian and Middle Eastern cuisines.
tapenade	A spread or condiment, usually consisting of puréed capers, olives, and anchovies in olive oil.
tartare	Often refers to a raw meat dish.
temper	To warm beaten eggs, by stirring a little of the hot ingredients into them, before adding the hot ingredients in entirety, so the eggs don't solidify.

truffle	A fungus that is cultivated primarily in France and Italy, valued for its earthy, aromatic nature.
truffle oil	Truffle oil is created when truffles are soaked in olive oil.
velouté	A stock-based white sauce, used as a base for other sauces.
Viognier; Vionnier	Intense, dry white wines with vibrant floral qualities and an intriguing bouquet with hints of apricots, peaches, and pears.
wasabi	Sometimes called Japanese horseradish, this green-colored condiment comes in paste and powder form.
water bath	A term indicating a container placed inside another container of water so the food cooks gently
wilted spinach/lettuce	Wilting spinach or lettuce, by steaming or drizzling hot liquid over them.
Zabaglione	A custard-like dessert made by whisking together egg yolks, wine and sugar.
zest	The brightly colored outermost skin layer of citrus fruit, removed with a zester, grater, or knife.

ABOUT THE PUBLISHERS

Chuck and Blanche Johnson started Wilderness Adventures Press, Inc. in 1993, publishing outdoor and sporting books. Along with hunting and fishing, they love fine dining, good wines, and traveling. They have always been able to "sniff out" the most outstanding and interesting restaurants in any city they visit.

On weekends, they experiment in the kitchen, cooking a variety of fish and meats, as well as preparing the harvest from their time in the field. This love of cooking has resulted in a large library of cookbooks, and has inspired them to create a series of cookbooks based on their love of travel and fine dining.

Chuck and Blanche make their home in Gallatin Gateway, Montana, along with their four German wirehaired pointers.

Photo Copyrights/Credits

Front cover, left to right across: ©Blanche Johnson; ©Blanche Johnson; ©David Mouton, Polara Studios; ©Blanche Johnson; ©David Mouton, Polara Studios; ©Blanche Johnson; ©Blanche Johnson; ©Il Piatto; ©Blanche Johnson; ©David Mouton, Polara Studios; ©Blanche Johnson; ©Il Piatto. **Back Cover, left to right across:** ©The Heathman; © John A. Rizzo, Rizzo Studios, Inc.; ©Basil Childers; ©Pambiche; ©Blanche Johnson; ©John A. Rizzo, Rizzo Studios, Inc.

All photos ©Blanche Johnson unless noted. **i:** Oregon Historical Society, #OrHi 26864. **vii-large:** ©Oregon Historical Society, #OrHi 38310. **vii-small:** ©Oregon Historical Society, #OrHi 12073. **x-large:** ©Oregon Historical Society, #OrHi 1027. **x-small:** ©Oregon Historical Society, #OrHi 5607. **7:** ©Carafe. **10:** ©Oregon Historical Society, #OrHi 66124. **12:** ©The Heathman. **24, 27:** ©Basil Childers. **30, 35:** ©Jake's Famous Crawfish. **38:** ©Oregon Historical Society, #OrHi 00711. **40:** ©Mother's Bistro. **47, 48, 49, 50, 52:** ©Pazzo Ristorante. **53, 54, 61, 63:** ©Basil Childers. **64:** ©A.H. Wulzer, panel 2 of 6, Oregon Historical Society, #OrHi 751a. **66, 67, 68, 69, 73:** ©Rizzo Studios, Inc., John A. Rizzo. **74:** ©Oregon Historical Society, #OrHi 25733. **86:** ©Oregon Historical Society, #OrHi 11984. **88:** ©Basil Childers. **93, 94:** ©andina. **96, 99:** ©Basil Childers. **102:** ©Oregon Historical Society, #OrHi 11736. **103, 104, 109:** ©Rizzo Studios, Inc., John A. Rizzo. **120:** ©Oregon Historical Society, #OrHi 24503. **122-top:** ©Lucy's Table. **126:** ©Lucy's Table. **128-top:** ©Paley's Place. **133:** ©Paley's Place. **138:** ©Oregon Historical Society, #OrHi 5569. **140-top:** ©Papa Haydn. **146:** ©Oregon Historical Society, #OrHi 5607. **147, 148, 151, 153, 154:** ©David Mouton, Polara Studios. **156-top:** ©Wildwood. **162:** ©Plainfield's Mayur. **178:** ©Oregon Historical Society, #OrHi 11937. **180, 181, 182:** ©Caprial's. **186, 188:** ©Castagna. **190:** ©Oregon Historical Society, #OrHi 13153. **191, 192, 193, 195, 196:** ©Il Piatto. **208:** ©Sala. **206, 207, 209, 211, 212:** ©Salvador Molly's. **213, 214, 215, 216:** ©Tucci.

Index

Notes

Notes

Notes